A History of ANN ARBOR

A History of
ANN ARBOR

Jonathan Marwil

THE UNIVERSITY OF MICHIGAN PRESS

Ann Arbor

First University of Michigan Press edition 1990
Copyright © 1987 by Jonathan Marwil
All rights reserved
Published in the United States of America by
The University of Michigan Press

1994   1993   1992   1991   4   3   2   1

Library of Congress Cataloging-in-Publication Data

Marwil, Jonathan, 1940–
    A history of Ann Arbor / Jonathan Marwil. — 1st University of
Michigan Press ed.
      p.   cm.
    Includes bibliographical references and index.
    ISBN 0-472-09463-7 (cloth : alk. paper). — ISBN 0-472-06463-0
(paper : alk. paper)
    1. Ann Arbor (Mich.) — History.   I. Title.
[F574.A6M35 1991]
977.4'35— dc20   90-25130
                                         CIP

To my brother William

CONTENTS

Acknowledgments   ix

Preface   xi

1 The Most Desirable Residence
   in the Great West: 1824–1851   1

2 A New Athens: 1851–1878   25

3 City of Knowledge and Homes: 1878–1914   55

4 The City Where Commerce and
   Education Meet: 1914–1945   93

5 Research Center of the Midwest: 1945–1980   135

   Illustrations   171

   A Note on Sources   175

   Notes   176

   Index   187

ACKNOWLEDGMENTS

In the summer of 1984 Don Hunt, then the publisher of the *Ann Arbor Observer*, commissioned this book. Although I am an historian of early modern Europe, the challenge of trying something different persuaded me to undertake the project.

In both the research and the writing I have gathered debts. The staffs at the University of Michigan's Bentley Historical Library (particularly Nancy Bartlett), the University of Michigan Library, the Ann Arbor Public Library, and the Burton Collection at the Detroit Public Library were invariably helpful. I am grateful as well to the *Ann Arbor News* for access to its photographic archive. Raymond Grew, John Shy, Thomas and Leslie Tentler, and Maris Vinovskis read the manuscript and offered excellent suggestions on how to improve it. Finally, I am indebted to the staff at the *Ann Arbor Observer*, especially Mary Matthews and Sharon Carney Solomon, for their skillful assistance.

Special thanks go to Dr. and Mrs. Harry A. Towsley for their help in underwriting the costs of producing this book.

Jonathan Marwil
June 1987, Ann Arbor

PREFACE

Thousands of years ago a retreating glacier sculpted the rolling landscape that would become Ann Arbor. Instead of withdrawing at an even pace and leaving behind the flat terrain found in much of southern Michigan, the glacier was occasionally made to pause by intervals of colder temperatures. Soon after the ice departed the first Indians arrived. They hunted, fished, and gathered the edibles nature freely provided, and in time began to cultivate crops. But the lingering evidence of trails reveals that many more Indians passed through this area than ever dwelled here, and even the Potawatami, whose territory it eventually became in the eighteenth century, had their homeland further west.

It was, then, to a wilderness crossroads of some beauty that the first white settlers came. Though already surveyed, it was as yet a wild place, where the only law was survival, the only rights those seized by creatures defining their territory, and the only history that composed by the cycles of nature. Before long, the settlers gave the place a name, put a price on the land, and made rules for each other. Thus Ann Arbor was born, and its history begun.

Knowing that history is important if one is to live in it wisely. Telling it requires several stories: of individuals and groups, of significant events and long-standing conditions, of recurrent dreams and earnest causes, and of an institution that brought pride, prosperity, and fame. No other city in the state, besides Detroit, is so well known or so often visited; no other city, including Detroit, has so completely fulfilled and maintained its identity. The very completeness of that identity distinguishes Ann Arbor even when it is compared to the four or five other significant university towns in America. Austin and Madison, for example, are state capitals; Cambridge and Berkeley lie geographically and psychologically within larger urban areas; New Haven has long existed apart from and even hostile to the university in its midst; and Princeton, while a university town par excellence, has its identity perhaps diminished by its very perfection. But if the University of Michigan has exercised the greatest influence over Ann Arbor's fortunes, the story of the city's development must still be told from its own perspective.

Anyone choosing to write its history is favored by an abundance of local records and newspapers, as well as by federal and state censuses, numerous collections of private papers, a growing body of memoirs, and a substantial archive of university materials. These would allow for a year-by-year chronicle of the city's progress, a long book of great, possibly overwhelming, detail. I have not written that book, nor have I chosen to tell the city's story by topic. Instead, I have tried within a short span to define the main lines of development, to evoke how and why people have lived here, and to examine issues and themes that seem important. Some of these will be unfamiliar because they have been undervalued or disregarded by previous writers whose love for the city inclined them to focus on its charms. Those charms are real and many, and public awareness of them—as well as the belief in Ann Arbor's exceptionality—has affected the city's development. But that development has primarily been shaped by such dour realities as geography, capital, fear, and inertia.

In addition to the written sources, there also exists a wealth of photographs stretching back to the Civil War, and their availability has prompted an unusual storytelling strategy. Relying principally on those photographs, but also on other graphic materials such as lithographs, maps, handbills, cartoons, and newspaper advertisements, I have tried to establish the narrative through images as well as through words. The reader, therefore, *must* heed the images, which are printed without captions; the text, sometimes only implicitly, will suggest how they are to be viewed. Gradually, the reader should realize their extraordinary potential for both discovering and telling the story of Ann Arbor, or any city. For they not only record what was seen (or thought) at some point in time, but how their creators and sponsors wanted themselves or their community to appear. The earliest lithograph of Ann Arbor, for example, renders a pastoral vision, not a real city, and in so doing expresses an idyllic sense of place and spirit felt by many citizens.

Though in purpose and method I depart from available treatments of the city's history, I have not disregarded them. Whatever their intentions and accomplishments, earlier writers have helped me define the story I tell. And this book, like theirs, will itself become not only a source for future searchers of the city's past, but a document of that past as well.

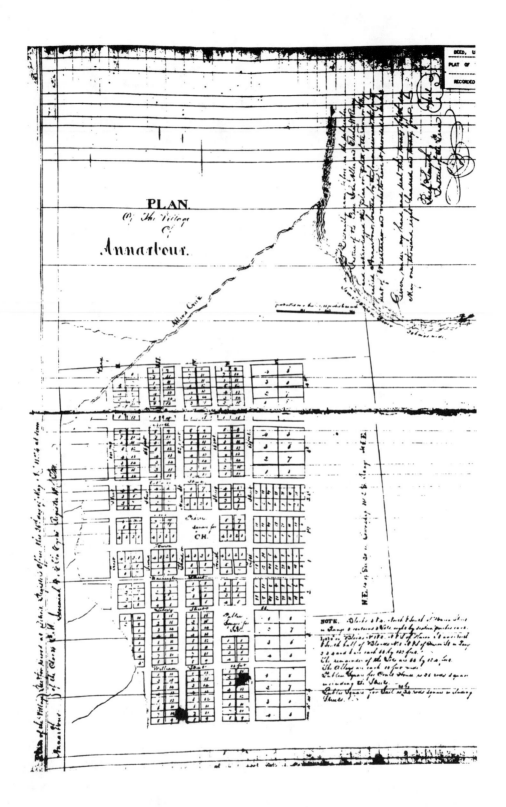

PLAN.
Of The Village
of
Annarbour.

Chapter 1

The Most Desirable Residence in the Great West

1824-1851

The first image of Ann Arbor is a sketch of a rectangle, nibbled at one corner, in which neatly drawn lots are intersected at right angles by streets. Slanting away from the nearby river is a creek that bends around the western border of the lots. Several tributaries run into it. The drawing is a plan registered in Detroit in May of 1824, some three months after the land for the village was purchased from the government. As a village plan, it resembles a hundred others; only the place names make it distinctive. Soon enough, shops and dwellings would rise up "without any regard to street lines" and beyond the edges of the plan, so that the symmetry of a pristine vision would give way to the irregularities of human choice and habit.

Before the plan and before the land purchase was the idea. Ann Arbor began in the minds of its founders, John Allen and Elisha Rumsey. They imagined a thriving community where once had been wilderness, and fresh futures to succeed their frustrating and mismanaged pasts. They thought also of the profits to be made when they sold the government lands they had purchased so cheaply ($1.25 an acre) for the site of their idea. Their dream of new opportunities and large profits was neither unique nor ignoble. Many other men were founding towns in the Midwest during the 1820s and 1830s, speculating that riches and respect would soon be theirs.

Allen and Rumsey were as new to each other as they were to the land they settled. They had met in Detroit in January of 1824, each having come to the Michigan Territory to purchase land and begin a new life. Behind each was a somewhat tattered reputation: Allen because of some bad debts in his native Virginia, Rumsey for deserting his family and misusing a loan in New York state. Shortly after meeting they left Detroit by sleigh, and early in February they chose a well-forested site along a creek that fed into a nearby river. The discovery of wood and water, essentials for development, ended their search. The cold of winter and the knowledge that they were already ten miles beyond the nearest settlement may also have influenced their choice.

Returning to Detroit, they registered their claim with the federal land office on February 14, 1824, Allen purchasing 480 acres, Rumsey 160. They chose a name for the site that acknowledged its generous stands of burr oaks, honored the common name of their wives, and beckoned evocatively—surely deliberately—to the tide of settlers expected in the territory. Annarbour, as it was then spelled, suggested a haven in an otherwise uncivilized landscape. Certainly it struck a more inviting chord than names like Allensville or Anapolis, which also seem to have been considered. Singular as a name, it retains to this day a subliminal enchantment.

By an 1821 law of the Michigan Territory, the proprietors of any new town had to "cause a true map or plat thereby to be recorded" before any lots could be offered for sale: thus the plan that Allen and Rumsey filed in Detroit "this 25th day of May A.D. 1824 at seven of the clock P.M." They filed it already confident of success, since the squares reserved for the courthouse and jail showed that the village had been designated the county seat. This was no small advantage to the two investors. Public institutions ensured that their paper village would one day prosper. Nor was it an advantage that had fortuitously fallen into their laps. They had lobbied for it, and, of course, paid a price: cash, labor, and materials in "the amount of one thousand dollars" for the construction of the courthouse and jail as well as a bridge over the Huron and the gift to the county of "such lots and parcels of ground" as were "deemed necessary for public uses." It was a price worth paying. More significantly, the transaction set a precedent. Within a few years, other men would be proposing similar deals to win even bigger prizes for Ann Arbor.

But even before Allen and Rumsey had filed their plat, people began arriving. By the first week of June upwards of a hundred lots were said to have been taken, with "several houses commenced [and] mechanics of almost all kinds on the spot." In the same week the two men placed a notice in the *Detroit Gazette* offering lots "on the most liberal terms, to persons desirous of permanently locating," especially "Mechanics and Artisans." The advertisement ran for several months while more people trickled into

2

the settlement. A large number of them were young—the 1827 census of Washtenaw County would show that almost half the white male population was under twenty-one—and many came from New York state. Allen's own family—wife, parents, children, and brother—made the journey up from Virginia, forsaking familiar lands and customs for difficult but hopeful circumstances.

Ever the enthusiast, Allen described Ann Arbor after a year as if it were the promised land. "Our water is of the purest limestone, the face of the country moderately uneven, our river the most beautiful I have beheld, and abounding with the most valuable fish, climate is as pleasant as tis possible to be, the river has not frozen entirely up this winter, the weather is as fine at this time as I have been accustomed to in April." Add to this many families "of the finest respectability," farms "which nature has provided already clear" for ploughing, roads being opened "in various directions," "mills of every kind started," and tradesmen readying for the "flood of emigrants expected next summer," and you had a community none could pass by. Only the "want of houses and barns" tarnished this roseate view, a want prominent in the remembrances of Dr. Benjamin Packard. Writing years later, he recalled that when he first visited the village in April of 1825, there were only eight crude houses and a debating club with two members, Allen and Rumsey.

A frontier community does not grow, however, by its style of architecture or leisure activities. Ann Arbor's future would depend on its economy—thus the purchase of the county seat and the call for artisans and mechanics—and that economy was initially centered on farming. The surrounding land, "already" cleared by a generous nature, was very suitable for planting and grazing, and before long it was being worked intensively and with an eye to large profits. The opening of the Erie Canal in 1825 not only eased the passage of settlers west, but cheapened markedly the shipping of goods east. By the 1840 federal census, Washtenaw County led the state in the production of barley and oats and in the number of horses and cattle. Sheep were also being raised in great numbers, foreshadowing the time when the county's herds would outrank every other east of the Mississippi.

Ann Arbor naturally stood to benefit from the prosperity of nearby township farmers. The village was where primary products were turned into usable commodities: wheat into flour and hides into leather, which in turn became shoes. By 1846 there were fifty-three coopers and fifty-six shoemakers in Ann Arbor, figures surpassed only by the number of carpenters. There were also three saw mills, two breweries, and a paper mill, all of them, like the flour mills and tanneries, depending on the running waters and tributaries of the Huron River and Allen's Creek.

Ann Arbor was also where farmers could store their wool and have implements repaired, and where they and their families could purchase necessities and baubles, consult a doctor or dentist, and obtain from a druggist or a saloonkeeper a concoction to improve their spirits. Often they had to barter for what they required, since money was in chronically short supply.

BREWERY.

THE Subscribers having made extensive additions to their Brewery, will in future be enabled to supply the public with superior strong Beer, and Table Ale, in quantities to suit purchasers.—Malt, Hops, Grains and Yeast, constantly on sale.

R. HOOPER & Co.

Ann Arbor Oct, 17th, 1833.

N. B.   All kinds of produce taken in payment.

But they were prosperous. In 1831, Lucy Morgan saw the average farmer growing "rich as fast as he pleases." Being the county seat, Ann Arbor was also visited by farmers who had legal work to be done: a deed registered, a sale drawn up, or a dispute settled. The court heard its first case in 1827, and by 1831, with a population of almost a thousand, the village had six attorneys. Twelve years later, with its population doubled, it had twenty-two.

This sizable host of legal talent lived off the land as surely as the farmer did. Both in the village and the county there was a steady traffic in real estate, and between sales, mortgages, disputes, and bankruptcies, a number of lawyers had the basis for a "comfortable" life. There was, of course, other work for lawyers, but if "Michigan fever" had not made of the state one vast land market primed for development in the 1820s and 1830s, the demand for lawyers would have been modest. One has but to glance at the notices in Ann Arbor's earliest paper, *The Western Emigrant*, to

4

realize how much property work was to be done. John Allen himself read for the law after founding Ann Arbor, and by 1831 he was a practicing attorney.

It was but one of Allen's many pursuits. He also served as postmaster, newspaper publisher, water company promoter, school organizer, village president, and tireless salesman of Ann Arbor's charms and advantages.

He directed his extraordinary energies toward ensuring the village's growth, believing that his own prosperity would necessarily follow. And he was right. A decade after founding the town, John Allen was living "like a prince in a magnificent house," selling for hundreds of dollars lots he had purchased for pennies, investing his and other people's money in projects promising bountiful returns, and perhaps already contemplating the move to New York City he would make in 1836 so as to better direct his financial affairs.

In those early years, however, Allen was not alone in his efforts to build the village, nor in realizing that what was good for himself was good for Ann Arbor. Anson Brown, owner of properties just north of the Huron in what was known as Lower Town, tried to shift the village's development to his side of the river, to streets whose names (Broadway, Wall) bespoke their creator's ambition. A fatal case of cholera put an end to his efforts in 1834. And there was Elijah Morgan, attorney, banker, landholder, and a principal figure in coaxing the state to situate the university in Ann Arbor. Others as well yoked their fortunes to the town. Some, like Brown and Elisha Rumsey, who died in September of 1827, did not live to achieve their dreams, but more than a few attained affluence and status.

A rather different figure was George Corselius, who arrived in Ann Arbor in 1829 at the age of twenty-three to take up the editorship of *The Western Emigrant*. His diaries, while maddeningly brief about village life, intimately reveal the hopes, ambitions, and disappointments of a man never quite at home in a frontier community. Like John Allen's wife, who eventually returned to Virginia, Corselius yearned for "something higher, better, finer, than I meet with here."

Besides editing the *Emigrant*, its successor, *The Michigan Whig*, and finally, the *Michigan State Journal*, Corselius helped found a lyceum and a debating club, served briefly as university librarian, and was active in the local temperance society. But these worthy activities neither brought him into the society of people he respected nor satisfied his questing spirit. He felt himself an outsider and solaced himself by undertaking various courses of study and envisioning books he should write. One by one these projects dissolved upon the effort, and Corselius cursed his "idleness" and lack of "diligence." He did, however, successfully read for the law while he was in Ann Arbor, and he imagined that being a lawyer would make him rich. But this vision too collapsed, perhaps because "I have been too sensitive and proud to elbow a way through a crowd—and such a crowd—to enter the lists and be distanced by the little sordid spirits that make up the competition in the game of life." Scarcely the view of a booster or mover, yet Corselius held on, feeling himself more at ease with "the ladies of Ann Arbor," whom he regarded as "more intelligent, and of a more dignified tone of character, than the men." He was in his own way a pioneer.

One more settler requires notice. In August of 1833 Friedrich Schmid arrived in Ann Arbor, two weeks shy of his twenty-sixth birthday and a few months removed from his ordination as an Evangelical Lutheran pastor. He had come to serve a group of Wuertemberg families living in and around Ann Arbor who several months earlier, on the initiative of Jonathan Henry Mann, "their patriarch," had petitioned the Lutheran seminary at Basel, Switzerland, for a spiritual leader. Their request had reflected the natural desire of a distinct and growing community to worship according to familiar forms. For several years Germans had been settling in Washtenaw County, particularly emigrants from the state of Wuertemberg. As yet their numbers were not large, but separated by language and customs from their English-speaking neighbors, they were inclined to act communally.

Schmid came to Ann Arbor with a missionary's instinct suitable to the needs of his flock. "There is," as he wrote to the elders at the Basel Seminary, "plenty of work here." Almost two dozen children, a few of them more than a year old, needed baptism, as did several older people, including some sixty years of age. "These are Germans whose parents emigrated to Pennsylvania and whose children grew up in the wilderness much like animals." Schmid first held services in a school, but in December the congregation began assembling in a meeting house built with their own hands in neighboring Scio Township and named Zion Church. A simple log building with large windows to let in light, it pretended to nothing except use. The people who gathered in it on Sunday to sing traditional German hymns and hear Schmid preach in their native Swabian dialect were no less frugal and practical in their outlook. Some were farmers, others shopkeepers and laborers. They had left a land of small holdings and limited opportunities and established home and church in a new but not dissimilar landscape. Though naturally pulled by memories and family to what they had known, they gradually adjusted to what they found, and they prospered. The letters they sent back would persuade others to follow; so, presumably, did bilingual booklets, like the *Emigrants' Guide to the State of Michigan*, which were distributed both in the German states and to immigrants landing in New York. But more convincing than words were the political and economic difficulties in the homeland itself, difficulties that following 1848 persuaded thousands of Germans to seek a new *Heimat*.

Thousands of Irish were seeking one as well, refugees from a famine of Biblical proportions. Those who settled in Ann Arbor usually had little but muscle and wit to make their way. Many of the men worked as laborers, numerous women and girls as servants. But not all the Irish were poor, especially those who had emigrated before the hard times. In the 1850 census we meet William O'Hara, a tailor, William McCreery, a leather dealer, and John Berry, an attorney, each with at least a couple of thousand dollars in property, not to mention several grocers, like Charles Hyland and Barry Haskins, with more modest holdings. The 1850 census also reveals that there were more Irish- than German-born residents in Ann Arbor Township, and thus presumably in the village itself. And in the person of Father Thomas Cullen, the local priest, they had a determined leader, a worthy counterpart to Pastor Schmid.

A few months before Schmid took up his duties in Ann Arbor, the Michigan Territorial Council passed a law incorporating the village, which by now also included land north of the Huron River. The 1833 act defined the offices and duties of town government, establishing a president, recorder, and six trustees, all of whom would sit as a village council, "to do all things which corporations of a similar nature can do to secure the peace, health, property, and prosperity of the inhabitants of said town." Specifically, the council had the power to make ordinances, tax property, regulate and improve the streets, and provide for such additional officers as were deemed necessary.

In theory there was much to do; in practice little was done in the early years, and that episodically. The council met monthly and in some months not at all if the president, who was responsible for calling meetings, chose not to, or was away. John Allen was selected as first president, and he held the early meetings in his office. The council's first ordinance took up the matter of hogs running at large; it was ordered that they be penned up at the owner's expense in public pounds. It seems hardly a solemn matter, unless one recognizes that hogs running about are dangerous—even today they are responsible for a number of injuries each year. Other ordinances passed at that first meeting—to prevent dogs running wild and firearms from being shot off— underscore the concern for safety, the first obligation of any government.

More feared than errant pigs and dogs or random gunshots was fire. Within hours it could reduce a village of log and frame structures to ashes. And thus by far the most comprehensive ordinance passed by the council during its early years was one that established procedures for preventing fires and organized a volunteer force to fight them. While other ordinances had two or three sections and filled a page of the council's minute book, the "Ordinance relating to a Fire Department," passed on December 12, 1836, ran to twelve sections and required seven pages.

Just how high a priority fire protection was given is evidenced in a subsequent appeal (January 8, 1837) to the legislature for a law exempting members of a fire department from serving in the militia and on juries, and from paying the poll tax. Such exemptions were a fair exchange for asking a man to risk his life as well as attend monthly meetings and purchase "a good and sufficient fire cap and coat." Actually, the village suffered only two major fires before the Civil War. One was in June of 1845, when the Michigan Central Railroad Depot and an adjacent warehouse were destroyed and "the whole of the lower town was in danger." The other (and worse) one was in April of 1849, when an entire block along Huron Street was destroyed.

But villagers always felt themselves vulnerable, and thus did not object to half their annual taxes going to fire protection. And if a traveling diorama showing what fire had done to a distant city a generation earlier exploited an all too human fascination, it also reinforced the determination not to allow "that dreaded element" to strike in their community.

8

COURT HOUSE !

Amusement for the Million ! !
FOR THREE NIGHTS!
Thursday, Friday and Saturday Evenings, Aug. 22d, 23d, & 24th.

The magnificent Diorama of the

CONFLAGRATION of MOSCOW

together with experiments in MAGIC and VENTRILO-
QUISM, by Mr. GESTER, will be exhibited as above.

ADMISSION TWENTY-FIVE CENTS.

Doors open at half past 7—to commence at 8 o'clock.

Less dramatic entertainments also visited the village. Almost yearly a circus or menagerie would arrive, and in the 1830s and 1840s traveling phrenologists regularly turned up to assay the craniums of the curious. John Allen once volunteered his head and was given a flattering report. Peddling a more certain image of oneself, however, were the traveling daguerreotypers who would set up shop for a few days and offer to "secure the shadow 'ere the form decays." Their instructions to interested parties—wear dark clothing or stripes, not light blue or pink—suggest how their surviving images have exaggerated the sober character of our ancestors' dress.

The gentleman who brought the "Conflagration of Moscow" to Ann Arbor was granted a license to exhibit by the council for a fee of $10. At the same council meeting permission was also given, for a fee of $3, to a group of Swiss bell-ringers to make their music for a single night. In the course of a year, these small sums—extracted from all promoters and entertainers willing to try their luck in Ann Arbor, and prorated to what the council guessed their audiences to be—added up. Together with the license fees required to sell alcoholic beverages and the taxes levied on property, they subsidized civic expenditures. Yet fifteen years after the village was incorporated, when it had grown to a population of about four thousand, the budget figures seem lilliputian: $556 raised by licensing fees, $1,596 by taxes on property—and most of what did not go to the Fire Department was distributed to townspeople in return for work on the streets, a never-ending labor.

But if village government was lean and irregular, it usually accomplished what the citizens demanded of it. A man was hired to ring the bell in the Presbyterian Church to mark the passing of the hours. Railings were built in front of the Exchange on Main Street to protect pedestrians from being "run over by stages and other carriages." Lamps were put up around the courthouse so that the significant village building would be illuminated. Committees frequently discussed how to achieve a larger water supply in the event of fire. Vaccinations were given to the poor at village expense when smallpox threatened. And anyone "intoxicated" publicly was apt to find himself up for trial. He was also apt to be taken aside and lectured privately about his habits, for temperance was vigorously preached in Ann Arbor.

The earliest issues of *The Western Emigrant*, begun in November of 1829, carried ads for a local temperance society. The paper itself, while in the hands of ardent temperance men John Allen and George Corselius, repeatedly editorialized against the evils of alcohol. So did the locally printed *Michigan Temperance Herald*, which had a brief life in 1838. What temperance meant for most people in those days was moderate use rather than abstinence; Corselius himself drank beer and hard cider, sometimes too much, and the *Emigrant* regularly published ads for local brewers and distilleries.

How significant a problem drinking actually was in early Ann Arbor is difficult to say. The local temperance society estimated that 12,455 gallons of whisky were consumed in 1830, but such a figure, given its source, must be suspect. Nonetheless, like any frontier community, Ann Arbor did not lack for grog shops. Stimulants, whether in the form of shows or drink, eased the tedium for which there was no radio or television, pains for which there were no drugs or therapy, and work from which there was no release until the grave. Drink-inspired mischief was common, and occasionally went beyond tipsy horsemen galloping down Huron Street. The damage done, for example, in the Presbyterian Church on the night of March 12, 1838—"some of the curtains of the desk, several of the lamps, and some trimmings of the pews wantonly destroyed"—sounds as if it might have been the work of some inebriate(s) rather than the "marauders" imagined by the citizens. In a credit ledger he kept on local businessmen in the 1840s and 1850s, Elijah Morgan cited several as "dissipated," but then Morgan was very active in the temperance cause, as was Dr. Benjamin Packard, who reported that during his first full year in Ann Arbor (1827-1828) a number of residents died of "delirium tremens."

On occasion, village government took a step for temperance beyond threatening those who imbibed unwisely. In 1844 it allowed the staging of a temperance drama "showing the different stages of a drunkard's life, from the commencement of fashionable drinking down to the lowest depths of degradation." Three years later it drew up what it described as a "Black List" of common drunkards to whom local merchants were forbidden to sell alcohol. Periodically new names were added. Though the list's effectiveness may be doubted, its creation suggests how deep the roots of temperance were embedded in a village that boasted three divisions of the Sons of Temperance and one of the Ladies of Temperance. In the decades following the Civil War, those roots would nourish a number of vigorous efforts to control drinking in Ann Arbor, efforts encouraged by the town's emerging identity as an educational place.

Meanwhile, newcomers continued to make their way to the settlement along the Huron, lured not only by glowing reports of relatives and friends, but by such advertisements as the "Map of the Village of Ann Arbor"—really an updated plat—which was published in New York City by Nathaniel Currier.

11

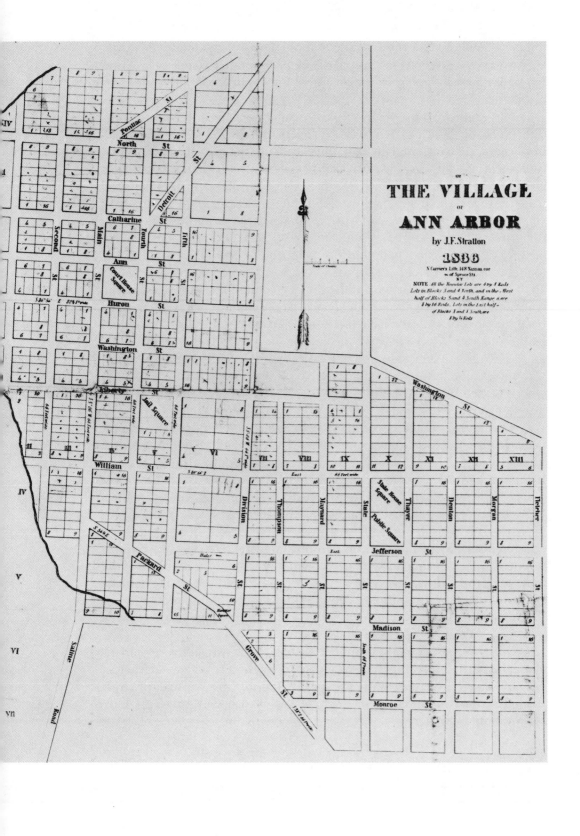

THE VILLAGE
OF
ANN ARBOR
by J.F.Stratton
1836
N Currier's Lith. 148 Nassau cor
of Spruce Sts.
BY
NOTE All the Regular Lots are 4 by 8 Rods
Lots in Blocks 3 and 4 North, and in the West
half of Blocks 3 and 4 South Range are
4 by 16 Rods. Lots in the East half
of Blocks 3 and 4 South, are
8 by 16 Rods

Drawn by Jonathan F. Stratton at the behest of the newly formed Ann Arbor Land Company, it was intended to stimulate further land purchases and settlement, particularly in the newly laid out plots east of State Street. Stratton was a trained surveyor, and so his precise rendering, accentuated by the printing, suggests a community ready for development. Diagonal streets now cut through the original rectangle, leading the eye to imagine further expansion. A State House Square is designated, witnessing the hopes of many villagers that Ann Arbor would win the looming competition for the state capital and thereby enhance its position.

In the eyes of the men whose names mark the eastward extension of the village, the prospects in 1836 of convincing the state to locate the capital in Ann Arbor appeared excellent. They had watched their village grow to rival in size and importance any town outside Detroit, and its central location established it as a natural meeting place. The very fact that the convention to consider statehood met in Ann Arbor that year underscored the role the village seemed destined to play, as had the appearance of a second newspaper the year before. With the railroad due soon, and talk growing of a second track to Monroe, further expansion seemed assured. The original plat of 1824 had announced a vision; the plat of 1836 argued a continuing and certain achievement.

And so it would be, despite the citizens eventually failing to win the state capital. Had they succeeded in capturing the much coveted honor, their community would have developed quite differently. So too might have Detroit, with a neighbor of such influence. But long before losing the capital, Ann Arbor had gained an even more glittering prize: the state university.

The prize did not come free. Several other communities vied for it, but the shrewd offer of forty free acres of town land on which to build the campus won Ann Arbor the site in March of 1837. Actually two sites had been offered: a hilly stretch on the north side of the Huron, and a flat tract east of State Street. The choice of the latter was more practical—and another blow to the development of Lower Town. The land proposal was made by the Ann Arbor Land Company, whose members realized that they and the town as a whole would profit from their calculated largesse. Hardly had the legislature approved the offer (March 20) than property began changing hands. Within a month, the *State Journal* (heir to the *Michigan Whig*, which had succeeded the *Western Emigrant*) noted that "speculation is in the full tide of successful operation. Our village, we trust, is destined to be the pride and ornament of Michigan." The discovery of gold along the Huron River could not have awakened greater hopes and enthusiasm. And in a very real sense, the villagers had made a strike, one that the responsible parties were eager to share with the world.

The early plats of Ann Arbor offer opportunities, but they scarcely exude the optimism of the notice published by the Ann Arbor Land Company in August of 1837. Distributed widely and published in newspapers, the notice was intended to draw new investment and new settlers to the village. Already a county seat and about to be home to a university, Ann Arbor seemed now to have unlimited potential. Indeed, no other document so dramatizes how land speculation shaped the town's early growth. The very clutter of its statement, which might have detracted from another kind of message, serves in this instance to communicate the ebullience and potential the company hoped to broadcast. And if fact gives way to hyperbole and even fantasy, there is so much optimism and good will about the message that the contemporary reader probably did not bother with its literal truthfulness. Both sellers and buyers of land knew how to fool themselves as well as others.

Though relatively few villagers immediately profited from land sales, there were already signs of how the arrival of the university would eventually benefit nearly all. "Our enterprising citizens," announced the *State Journal*, "have already commenced purchasing sites and making calculations for erecting numerous dwelling houses." Those houses, and the buildings to follow, would employ many in their construction and use.

As an impetus to growth and progress, therefore, the university was eagerly awaited. Some villagers, though, also anticipated its civilizing promise. Ann Arbor in the mid 1830s was still very much a "raw . . . settlement," a collection of log and frame buildings interspersed with a few built of brick and crisscrossed by mud streets. Travelers complained of difficulty in procuring "decent accommodations" and an ordinance had to be passed forbidding the watering of animals at the courthouse well. Its cultural condition was little better. Such efforts as the Allen and Rumsey debating society, or the lyceum organized in 1831 and then reorganized in 1834, did not attract many residents. Neither did the reading society George Corselius attended in 1833 nor the Young Men's Literary Society that was activated in 1836. And bookselling, a side venture of Corselius, also failed to thrive.

Even basic education was slighted. A number of schools had begun in the first ten years, but their life span was usually only a year or two. The problem was not a lack of competent teachers or civic leadership. John Allen was a driving spirit behind at least two schools, and he seems to have persuaded the secretary of the Michigan Territory, William Woodbridge, to send his son from Detroit to Ann Arbor to be educated. The problem lay instead with the parents, who were either unwilling or unable to pay the necessary fees. In 1832 little more than a fifth of the children in Ann Arbor between the ages of five and fifteen were attending school. "Too long," moaned the *State Journal* in September of 1835, "have our citizens *slept* on this subject. They need the power of some galvanic battery applied to their slumbering faculties, to arouse them from their fatal lethargy."

The decision eighteen months later to locate the university in Ann Arbor provided the necessary charge. It is no coincidence that the longest enduring private school, the Misses Clark School for Young Ladies, was established in 1839, two years after the regents' decision. Or that in the 1840s the presence in "our midst" of an "able and learned faculty" prompted renewed citizen efforts to organize cultural societies.

The university promised a significant future for Ann Arbor, a dependable influx of immigrants through whose presence the village would prosper economically, culturally, and architecturally. But villagers still looked to the farmland of the county for their prosperity; the spring wool clip and autumn harvest mattered more than yearly enrollments of six or seven dozen students. Almost four out of five adults in the county worked in agriculture, and the "out lots" and "improved farms" offered by the Ann Arbor Land Company indicated how rurally focused the village was. So too did the crafts and industries that employed a majority of villagers. It followed, then, that agricultural news filled the local newspapers—whose very names suggested a countywide perspective—and that the first county fair as well as the first permanent fair site were located in the village. Those farmers who attended that first fair in 1848 were perhaps a little awed by the new university buildings,

but Ann Arbor still seemed to them, as to most of its inhabitants, much more a market center than a university town.

Most newcomers would have agreed, whether they had come from New York or New England, still the principal sources, or Ireland, the German states, or Canada. The last supplied a steady stream of immigrants to the area and the largest percentage of foreign-born to the state as a whole as late as 1880. Although alumni organizations like the New England Society

16

and the New York Society were formed, and old home memories kept alive by charitable gestures,

---

NOTICES.

Relief for the Suffering People of IRELAND.

The Executive Committee hereby give notice that a Depot for Provisions has been established at Gen. Clark's warehouse, and that contributions in Flour, Pork &c., will be received and forwarded free of storage. Contributions in Cash, may be made to either of the undersigned at their offices, or to either of the Soliciting Committee, whose names will be found in the published proceedings of the meeting held Feb. 27, 1847.

Flour. fine or super fine, Pork, Flour bbls. and Pork do. are wanted.

> D. M'INTYRE,
> GEO. SEDGWICK,   Executive
> C. CLARK,
> WM. O'HARA,   Committee.
> E. CLARK,

Ann Arbor, March 3, 1847.

---

the various immigrant groups were more or less absorbed into the Ann Arbor community within a few years.

Not so the Germans. They learned English but kept their native tongue and made sure their children learned it. They joined local groups and entered politics, but they prayed in their own churches, gathered in their own service organizations, formed their own band, and established their own volunteer fire complany (Relief), which drew the admiration of their Yankee neighbors. Assimilated and much respected for their industry and public spirit, they nonetheless retained for decades a separate identity as well.

Some villagers in the 1840s, however, resented the arrival of so many foreigners. Like a significant number of their countrymen during this period, they viewed the immigrant from abroad as a danger to cherished principles and institutions he was unlikely to value or understand. This resentment was directed particularly at Catholics, who were alleged to be obedient to the dictates of the Roman Church and thus incapable of acting as independent voters. In Ann Arbor the only sizable Catholic population were the Irish, whose status had been solidified in 1845 with the completion of the first brick church (St. Thomas) in the village. Even though the German community was largely Protestant, its distinctly foreign character also made it suspect in the eyes of those who feared the alien incursion.

How threatened either immigrant group actually felt is not clear. But those who questioned their allegiance, primarily Whig supporters, were exercised enough in the aftermath of Polk's victory in 1844 to form the Native American Association of Ann Arbor early in 1845. Dedicated to limiting the flow of immigrants into the county and to extending to twenty-one years the required period of residence prior to naturalization, the association was largely the creation of Edward Fuller, a former Whig state senator known for his oratory. A year later the group started up a newspaper, the *Ann Arbor American*, which lasted only a few months and ran a candidate for township supervisor who fared badly. Converts to the cause were few, perhaps because there was no real evidence for its fears. "Do we find," asked the Democratic *Michigan Argus*, "our Catholic neighbors in Washtenaw County plotting the overthrow of our government?" Or perhaps because local Whigs not only held a solid majority in village politics—Henry Clay had won Ann Arbor in 1844—but had traditionally been ready to reach out for immigrant support, and in the case of the Germans were confident of bringing them "into the right political path."

Though the widespread national surge of hostility toward foreigners had little effect in Ann Arbor, a warning voice in the Native American Association's articles—"All such as are bound by an allegiance lying back of, and superior to their allegiance to this Government, should be watched with the argus eyes of a neversleeping Jealousy"—would be heard again during World War I, with far greater menace and consequences.

But in the 1840s a visitor to Ann Arbor would have seen more signs of growth and vitality than of community dissension. The first university buildings had gone up, several new churches beckoned worshipers, and blocks of brick stores were beginning to replace frame structures. Although money was still sometimes scarce, the community's economy was well on its way to recovery from the hard times following the nationwide Panic of 1837. Hopes were high that Ann Arbor might become a major manufacturer of woolen cloth instead of merely an embarkation point in the passage of raw wool to the great mills in the East. There were clear signs too—with several presses and a paper mill already in place—that in addition to a seat of learning the village would also be a center of the printing industry.

Alive with commercial schemes, Ann Arbor was expanding in size and population. In 1845 the county census had arrived at a population of 3,030; five years later, thanks largely to an 1846 charter amendment extending boundaries, the federal census found over 4,000 inhabitants. Of these, a large number were school-age children. During the 1840s the newspapers no longer carried stories bewailing "boys from 5-16 running about our streets imbibing idle and vicious habits." They and their sisters were now more apt to be safely seated in the two public schools or the several private and parochial academies. There, in the words of Huck Finn, one of their contemporaries, they were being "sivilized." A few may even have signed up for the dancing school proposed to open in the autumn of 1846 "as soon as a sufficient number of scholars can be obtained."

Many children, however, never reached the age to enroll in school. The mortality statistics for Ann Arbor Township recorded in the 1850 census tell a sad if familiar story: of the sixty-seven people who had died in the past year, twenty-two were a year old or younger, and an additional thirteen were under the age of sixteen. "Those diseases," commented the enumerator, "which are most common are ague and bilious fevers: Those most fatal dysentery and congestive brain fever."

In other years cholera and smallpox had carried off numerous villagers. When one of these terrifying diseases reached Ann Arbor the authorities took what measures they could. In the autumn of 1848 the village council, upon learning of two cases of smallpox, rented a house belonging to Solomon Mann and converted it into a temporary pest house where the sick could be attended to. Over the next several months village funds were paid out to doctors, attendants, and, ultimately, coffin-makers. And in May of 1849, when word of cholera reached the village, the authorities took steps "to disarm the disease of its terror should it come among us" by appointing a "Board of Health" to examine "all nuisances" in the village.

Such measures were taken to protect the inhabitants. But efforts were also made to preserve the reputation of the village as a safe place. Once an area was thought to be unhealthy—an early impediment to the development of the Michigan Territory as a whole—prospective settlers would go elsewhere. That is why local newspapers in 1846 had quickly trounced reports that "our village is unhealthy," and why from the very beginning promotional literature had emphasized Ann Arbor's "healthy and delightful situation" and its "salubrious climate." There was no escaping or denying the presence of "ague and bilious fevers" (which we know to have often been malaria), but the problem subsided as the land was cleared and the swamps drained. Meanwhile, the telegraph line, opened between Detroit and Ann Arbor on Christmas Day in 1847, provided early warning of the approach of more lethal plagues.

Mortality listings cover two pages in the 1850 federal census; the other hundred-odd pages describe the living and are a rich source of information. A single page is suggestive.

SCHEDULE I.—Free Inhabitants in _Ann Arbor_ in the County of _Washtenaw_ State of _Michigan_ enumerated by me, on the _17th_ day of _July_ 1850. _Jeremiah Peek_ Ass't Marshal. 534

Dwelling-houses numbered	Families numbered	The Name of every Person whose usual place of abode on the first day of June, 1850, was in this family.	Age	Sex	White, Black, or Mulatto	Profession, Occupation, or Trade of each Male Person over 15 years of age	Value of Real Estate owned	Place of Birth, Naming the State, Territory, or Country	Married within the year	Attended School within the year	Persons over 20 who cannot read & write	Whether deaf and dumb, blind, insane, idiotic, pauper, or convict	
331	331	Charles Dulla	42	m		Merchant	1500	Mass					1
		Caroline Do	44	f				Vermont					2
		Celia Do	6	m				Mich		1			3
		Geo Do	3	m				Do					4
		Garrett Babcock	17	f				Do					5
332	332	Wm S. Maynard	48	m		Merchant	50000	Mass					6
		Julia G Do	48	f				New York					7
		Julia G Do	20	f				Do					8
		Alice Do	18	f				Mich		1			9
		Mary Do	16	f				Mich		1			10
		Cornelia Do	13	f				Do		1			11
		Frances E Do	6	f				Do		1			12
		Helen I Do	4	f				Do					13
		Lana Harra	20	f				Germany					14
		Henry Clay	25	m	½			Kentucky					15
		Nicholas Obrien	17	m				Mich		1			16
333	333	W H Ramsdell	35	m		Attorney	5000	New York					17
		Mary Do	28	f				Do					18
		Ellen Howard	20	f				Ireland					19
		Solomon Mann Jr	23	m		Do		New H					20
334	334	Hiram Becker	47	m		Merchant	10000	New York					21
		Sophia Do	46	f				Vermont					22
		Chas Do	20	m		Student		New York					23
		Edwin Do	19	m		Do		Do					24
		Julia Do	17	f		Do		Do					25
		Mary Do	12	f				Do		1			26
		Fred k Do	6	m				Mich		1			27
		Mary Phillips	18	f				Pa					28
		Catherine Becker	28	f				New York					29
335	335	Fred k Smith	43	m		Lockman Mc	4000	Germany					30
		Louisa Do	38	f				Do					31
		Emanuel Do	15	m				Mich		1			32
		Louisa Do	13	f				Do		1			33
		Fred k Do	11	m				Do		1			34
		Mary Do	9	f				Do		1			35
		Sophia Do	7	f				Do		1			36
		Elizabeth Do	5	f				Do					37
		Johnetta Do	2	m				Do					38
		Timothy Do	4/12	m				Do					39
		Christena Fisle	28	f				Germany					40
336	336	Will Aldham	48	m		Gardner	200	England					41
		Anna Do	46	f				Do					42

Consider, for example, William S. Maynard, listed here as a merchant, but a considerable land developer as well. His father, Ezra, had been among the earliest settlers, and William himself, once he arrived, had obviously prospered. This can be seen not only in his $50,000 real estate holdings, but in his having at least two servants, a German girl (Lana Harra) and a black man (Henry Clay), in his elegant home on Main

20

Street. The "Fred Smith" found in the lower part of the page is, of course, Pastor Friedrich Schmid, now married to a daughter of Jonathan Henry Mann and father of eight children whose care was partially in the hands of Christena Figle, a servant.

Many other families also had servants, often young Irish or German women, and the availability of domestic work in the prospering community is one reason why the number of females was growing. By the 1860 census they would comprise a majority of the population. Also noteworthy is that virtually all of the children of school age had been attending school. While a census page from a working-class area would disclose a different pattern, school attendance was now the rule rather than the exception.

Finally, the federal census indicates what the state census report of 1854 would confirm: that the population of the village was still comparatively young. More than 80 percent of the males were under forty-five years of age, and more than 80 percent of the females were under forty. Children under ten made up more than 20 percent of the total population. The village had its elders, primarily individuals who had decided to join sons and daughters once settled. But it would be at least another decade before the natural cycle of maturation would establish a population profile similar to the eastern and European communities from which the settlers had come. "We who have just come to this State," University of Michigan President Henry Tappan told an Ann Arbor audience in 1852, "meet every day with the old settlers who are not yet old men."

On July 4, 1850, the citizens of Ann Arbor held a giant celebration. The festivities began with a salute of thirteen guns and the ringing of bells, followed by a procession through the streets, a reading of the Declaration of Independence, and a commemorative oration. Then, under a bower erected in the public square, a sumptuous dinner was held, climaxed by numerous toasts and a further salute of thirty guns. Left to the evening hours were a fireworks display together with the release of two large "illuminated Balloons." This was a celebration "in the old fashioned way," the likes of which had not been seen in many years. In earlier days the "anniversary of our National Independence" had been a vital event, a day on which the villagers' sense of their own emergence as a community could be affirmed within the memory of the nation's. But as the years had passed, and "worldly pursuits" flourished, such testimonies to the significance of the Fourth no longer seemed necessary.

A highlight of the 1850 ceremonies was the appearance in a carriage of two "surviving heroes of the revolution," one of them ninety-six years old, brought out to recall sacrifices made long ago. But the toasts after dinner looked forward as well. There was a lifting of glasses to the preservation of the Union, to Hungary and her fight for freedom, and to California, "the land of sunset, golden and glorious.'' Those words had a decided immediacy, for a number of villagers had already gone to California, and dozens more would soon follow. Among those already lured west were John Allen and George Corselius, each pursuing yet another dream of success, and failing. Corselius died in May of 1849, en route back to New York from Panama, having decided that his health would not stand the further journey to El Dorado. Allen at least reached the gold fields, and in July of 1850 was to be found prospecting on the Mercedes River. But in the autumn, having little to show for his efforts, he forsook mining and took up growing vegetables on a twenty-acre plot outside of San Francisco. There, cultivating his garden, he was happy. This newest enterprise was short-lived, however. On March 11, 1851, the principal founder of Ann Arbor died, according to a newspaper account, ''among strangers,'' after a long illness.

News of Allen's death reached Ann Arbor at the end of April in the wake of a more significant event. On April 4 the state legislature had passed an act incorporating Ann Arbor as a city, divided into four wards and governed by a mayor and an eight-member common council. With this new charter came an enlarged taxing authority and thus greater capacity to provide for ''an efficient fire department''—still the citizens' key priority—as well as adequate streets and sidewalks. Also granted was the power ''to organize, maintain, and regulate a police of the city,'' a power obviating the need for citizen vigilante groups like the Mutual Protection Society, formed in 1845 for ''the detection of thieves and the recovery of stolen property.'' The prospect of higher taxes, although displeasing to the ''pennywise,'' was overwhelmingly accepted by the citizens. Living in the ''second town in wealth and population in the state,'' they were ready to face up to the obligations as well as the benefits of growth.

Enthusiasm for the new charter peaked when George Sedgwick, the primary figure in its formulation and passage, arrived back from Lansing with the document in hand. A large crowd gathered at the depot, and when the train pulled in ''three hearty cheers went up, that made the Welkin ring,'' while the German Brass Band kept pace with rousing music ''in honor of our emergence from confusion and disorganization, into the hope of 'better times coming.' '' The following Monday Sedgwick was elected mayor by a huge majority. Two days later, at the first meeting of the council, Alderman Elijah Morgan moved that ''the Recorder be authorized to procure a suitable book in which he shall record all the proceedings and bylaws of the Common Council.'' A new beginning demanded such a gesture. But the old Minute Book, freshly paginated, was retained instead, nicely symbolizing how close the ties between past and future would be. The gesture also represented thrifty habits that would long endure.

No less enduring would be Ann Arbor's fame as a "lovely city." Words describing its beauties and benefits were already far-flung; images would follow, like the lithograph done by Robert Burger in 1853. The view is from the northwest, with the Huron on the left and the line of trees in the center running along Allen's Creek. In the far distance are the university buildings, foreshadowing in their scale how education will eventually define the community's development.

But what stands out in this scene is the larger perspective of human achievement in harmony with nature. We see Ann Arbor through a sylvan setting, as a peaceable kingdom of foliage and sheep. The artist has carefully polished the primary elements of the city and composed them into an idealized perspective. What viewer would not be pleased to live in such a place? Ann Arbor is captured here as, indeed, "the most desirable residence in the Great West," clean, healthy, beautiful, and prosperous, a city attractive to men and women of any purpose or persuasion. It is the place that John Allen had envisaged, that the Ann Arbor Land Company had promoted, and that its citizens imagined—more or less—they inhabited.

Chapter 2

A New Athens

1851–1878

This map of Ann Arbor, a single panel of a much larger survey of Washtenaw County, was published in 1856. Settlement is understandably still concentrated within the original 1824 plat, but already there is a wide scattering of structures east of Division, not the least of which is the new Union School on State Street—here labeled University Avenue—between Washington and Huron. West of Allen's Creek, along streets that ran at angles to avoid the low ground of the creek's tributaries, there are also a number of buildings. By comparison, Lower Town, its quarter-century-old thoroughfares gaping with empty lots, is in a state of suspended development, waiting still to be incorporated within its former rival. And as yet, there is only a trace of building south of the university, and no trace at all, because of the map's dimensions, of the old fairgrounds south of Hill where in September of 1850 the city had hosted the state fair.

Across numerous properties run the names Maynard and Morgan, evidence of the interest these two men continued to have in a city that Maynard, as mayor-elect in April of 1856, saw as having a splendid future. Few townspeople would have disagreed with his prophecy, certainly none of the men who had subscribed to the survey and thus had been listed in the "References and Business Directory." Many of them were Germans, including August Widenman, alleged to have originally come to Ann Arbor to serve as a local German consul. One who was not German, W. F. Spaulding, owned a marble works on Huron Street where tombstones were carved for Ann Arbor's several cemeteries.

One of these, the "private cemetery" north of the university, was the burying ground of the small community of Jews who had settled in the city in the preceding decade. Their numbers were modest, perhaps fifty, certainly less than one hundred, and many were connected by marriage. Most prospered, particularly the nucleus of this community, the five Weil brothers, leather merchants and dealers in wool and furs, who by the end of the Civil War operated the biggest business in Ann Arbor. The Weil family was originally from Bohemia. Solomon, the first of the brothers to settle in Ann Arbor, arrived in 1845, and the others, along with their parents, followed. The father, Joseph, acted as rabbi for the religious services which were regularly held in a brick house on West Washington Street. The success of the Weils and of other Jews, like Charles Fantle, who ran a dry goods business, and Simon Guiterman, who with Samuel Sykes started a clothing business in 1851 that eventually expanded to Detroit, Dexter, and Jackson, was generally respected. But not always.

OPPOSITION TO JEWS!

WM. OHARA respectfully informs the inhabitants of Ann Arbor and vicini that he has just returned from the city of New York, with a large and well selected Stock of Cloths; Cassimeres. Satinettes, Vestings, Overcoatings and Trimmings, which he will sell cheaper than any other house in the city, having no rents or clerk hire to pay, and determined not to be undersold by any. All he requires is a call before purchasing elsewhere; and as for his work, hi customers have had a good chance of testing it, for 12 years back. You will bear in mind that those goods are none of the Eastern Shelf-worm

Slop Work,

Such as is brought into this market and sold for good stock, which creates a prejudice against Ready Made Clothing, where people are deceived. These are all fresh from the Importers, and all made under the supervision of the subscriber, and

Warranted not to R ip.

This ugly advertisement directed at Sykes and Guiterman may have been only the edge of a more widespread resentment. Still, other sources, such as Elijah Morgan's blunt ledger entries and the local newspapers, generally describe individual Jews admiringly. And in 1859 and again in 1860, Jacob Weil was elected alderman for the Second Ward. In the latter year he was also considered as a possible candidate for mayor, but his decision to move to New York ended his Ann Arbor career. He resigned his seat on the council in November of 1860 and presumably had left the city before the Washington Birthday parade of 1861, in which his father, tall and spry at eighty-four, marched as captain.

No site or structure on this 1856 map, however, marks the presence of the blacks living in Ann Arbor before the Civil War. From a handful in 1830, their numbers had grown to over eighty by 1860, with another two dozen living across the river in Lower Town. Few had any property, according to the census, and some could not read or write, but they were a visible, acknowledged presence, able to sustain a church on Fuller Street and to earn modest livings with the work of their hands. John Freeman and Thomas Freeman—the latter a delegate to the 1843 state convention of Colored Citizens of Michigan—ran barber shops that advertised regularly in the local papers; James Brook was a drayman with real and personal property valued at $2,500, a not inconsiderable sum; and Henry Clay, whom we met earlier in W. S. Maynard's household, set himself up in 1854 "to do whitewashing in all its branches." Two years later he was still at it, and using an engaging wit to find customers.

Whitewashing was not one of those ''mechanical arts'' that Thomas Freeman had urged blacks to learn so as to prosper and gain ''equal political rights.'' And some readers of the *Argus* probably fumed at Clay's mocking what blacks as yet had no part in: the university and elections. But other readers, like the over two hundred Washtenaw County residents who petitioned the state constitutional convention in 1850 to extend the franchise to blacks, would have praised his marketing spirit. For while the community had its quietly dignified racists and outspoken bigots—''now commences the worship of the nigger'' cried a hostile onlooker at an abolitionist meeting in January of 1861—it also had many men and women of more tolerant views, and a pocket of staunch abolitionists. The presence of these more enlightened citizens explains why Ann Arbor had been the birthplace of the Michigan Anti-Slavery Society in 1836, the home of the abolitionist *Signal of Liberty* in the 1840s, a center of no small support for the presidential bids of James Birney (Liberty Party) in 1844 and Martin Van Buren (Free Soil) in 1848, a common stop for anti-slavery lecturers (white and black) in the 1850s, and a way station for fugitive slaves.

As the eye wanders over the 1856 map of the city, seeking out evidence of change and growth, it keeps being pulled back to the site of the university, much as the town itself was inevitably being drawn to the institution. Thus far the gravitational effect was weak, for though the space allotted to the campus was large, and the new (1851) medical department generating substantial enrollment increases, the number of students and faculty was small, both absolutely and in proportion to the townspeople. In 1856 there were some four hundred students and twenty faculty members, their numbers combining to less than 10 percent of the town's population. Twenty-five years later, having increased sevenfold, students and faculty represented 35 percent of the residents, many of whom realized that the university had become the controlling force in their community's destiny.

Critical to the emergence of the institution was Henry Philip Tappan, who arrived in Ann Arbor as president in 1852 determined to create the first real university in America. Absorbed by the Prussian ideal of the university as a place where professors conducted original research, taught by lecture, and trained graduate students, Tappan set about, as he announced in his inaugural address, to establish ''a new Athens'' along the Huron. New faculty were brought in, new buildings went up, and a new sense of purpose infused the campus, as Tappan, pointing to the example of Berlin, sought to prove that ''a great university may be of rapid growth.'' Not since John Allen in his prime had Ann Arbor known a man of such vigor and purpose bent on shaping reality to a vision. And like Allen, Tappan was commanding in presence, confident to the point of arrogance, and eloquent. When he strode about the streets, one of his Saint

Bernards at heel, he struck even those beyond his rule as the embodiment of authority.

Tappan's impact on Ann Arbor went far beyond the force of his personality. In his inaugural address he emphasized how a community benefited from the presence of a university.

A great university, too, in any place, by its direct expenditures, by the numbers which it brings together, by the industry which it calls into action in its necessary going on, is an important element of commercial prosperity, besides all the collateral and consequential commercial benefits. . . The city of Edinburgh is a city of one hundred and fifty thousand inhabitants. Its University is the foundation of all its prosperity. Take that away, and it would sink into comparative insignificance. New Haven in our own country affords another illustration of the same kind.

Hearing this, some in his audience probably thought he exaggerated. But they may have begun to change their minds a few minutes later when they heard Tappan ridicule the American habit of erecting ''vast dormitories for the night's sleep, instead of creating libraries and laboratories for the

29

day's work.'' This was a hint that the university would be relinquishing its hitherto accepted responsibility for housing students. A year later, in his report to the regents, Tappan developed the hint into a policy, arguing that the dormitory system was not only wasteful of university resources but ''objectionable in itself'' because it often led students to ''contract evil habits'' and engage in ''disorderly conduct.''

Another three years would pass, however, before the regents were persuaded to appoint a committee to determine if ''board and rooming accommodations can be obtained in town at reasonable rates.'' They could be, and in September of 1858 the university steward put notices in the local papers telling citizens ''desiring to take boarders during the coming college year'' to contact him. At first neither demand nor supply was great, but as the number of students increased, the housing and feeding of them became a primary source of income for dozens of citizens and a secondary source for hundreds more.

Tappan's claim that Ann Arbor would accrue ''vast and vital'' benefits from the university was matched by his assumption that the city should stand as a ready benefactor to the university, which still subsisted primarily on the lease or sale of federally granted lands. ''Nothing would give him greater pleasure,'' he told a gathering of citizens in January of 1853, ''than to observe alcove after alcove in our . . . university well filled with books and surmounted with the donor's name.'' The wish opened a number of wallets, with such notables as James Kingsley, W. S. Maynard, Elijah Morgan, and George Sedgwick each contributing $100. In all, $1,565 was raised, enabling Tappan during his subsequent trip to Europe to ''make some very valuable and advantageous purchases of books.''

A more substantial request for funding came in December of 1859, when the regents decided to ask the citizens for $10,000 to erect a building for the new law department. The conduit for the request was the Ann Arbor Bar, and a meeting of citizens in March of 1860 voted to raise the money. To stiffen their resolve, one regent hinted that certain ''Detroit gentlemen'' hoped to capture the law department for ''their city.'' Six months later the regents had obtained ''assurances'' from the Bar that the ''subscriptions'' for the $10,000 ''will very soon be filled,'' and in March of 1861 the regents had ''reason to believe'' that the money was ''ready to be advanced.'' Their hopes proved false, however, and the regents eventually paid for the building out of their own resources.

Why the money was not raised is a mystery. Perhaps the law department's ''removal'' seemed improbable; perhaps the amount to be raised, once the Civil War began, seemed impracticable. No evidence survives to show that the matter was ever brought before the common council, let alone the taxpayers. If it had been, the chances of success would have been small. The city, by its charter, could not have incurred such a debt without permission of the legislature, and the building itself would probably not have seemed vital enough to warrant seeking such permission. Soon enough the community would be willing to give the university large sums of money for building, but only for structures, primarily hospitals, seen as enhancing the citizens' welfare as well as the university's interests.

Pride as well as pragmatism formed the townspeople's view of the university during its early years. In their midst was an institution that promised to become the "ornament of the state." Could Jackson say that about its prison, Kalamazoo about its asylum, or even Lansing about its capitol? Was not the education of its citizens the noblest responsibility of the state? When they strolled by the first buildings, curious townspeople sensed that within those stark edifices something important was happening,

and something that made the town important. Some of them also felt that the university offered an opportunity—tantamount to a responsibility—to improve the cultural life of Ann Arbor. And so the newspapers summoned townspeople to hear the prominent speakers brought in by the Student Lecture Association—"Our city is no longer to be behind the times in the matter of popular lectures." Or intimated that the "able and learned faculty" should be drawn upon to assist and support local cultural organizations. With such promptings it was not long before townspeople gladly acknowledged the value-shaping influence of the university as well as its integral economic role. Large numbers of them turned out in August of 1845 to watch the first eleven students graduate, and for many years after, commencement day was both an unofficial civic holiday and an occasion for Ann Arbor residents to affirm an "interest" in the institution, an interest no less vital, as they saw it, than that of the students and faculty.

To be thus valued is also to be possessed, and the townspeople, even before Tappan's arrival, revealed just how proprietary they could feel about the university. In December of 1849 the faculty expelled twenty-two students for belonging to fraternities, membership in which had been forbidden. As the number represented almost half of the total enrollment, and the action appeared draconian, many townspeople were upset.

It was a "large and crowded" gathering, one that heard students and townspeople alike express their complaints. Several resolutions were unanimously passed, among them one that claimed the right of the citizens "to take great interest in the welfare of our university," and another that asserted rather more:

> That in the prosperity of the university depends, in a great degree, the prosperity of our village; and hence it is not only our right but our duty to look to the manner in which its affairs are managed.

Thus enunciated, the claim assumes an authority impossible to define, let alone exercise. Yet it follows naturally from the supportive stance previously welcomed by the university. And though many other townspeople backed the faculty's decision to expel, and signed a petition to that effect, they did not challenge the principle that the citizens had a responsibility to examine the university's activities.

They could hardly have been expected to think otherwise. A group of citizens had donated the land on which the university was built, and the community as a whole welcomed its presence and offered assistance when requested. In the minds of many the university was a long-term investment, to be watched over and nurtured. It stood as excellent collateral for

32

other ventures and returned steady dividends. Thus institutional decisions that might jeopardize its welfare or reputation, like the expulsion of the students, most of whom never returned, or the unexplained firing in 1854 of J. Adams Allen, a well-respected professor in the medical department, became matters of community concern.

While some people disapproved of "too great a disposition . . . to censor the actions of the officers of the university," few questioned the right of the citizens to act as a watchdog. After all, was not the "welfare" of every "farmer, mechanic, trader, or professional man . . . interwoven with it?" But however self-serving or intrusive citizens were, they were also proud of the university, and able to value properly, more or less, what it was about. In brief, theirs was a complex response to an institution that affected their lives in complex ways.

The university awakened pride and respect; its neighbor, the Union School, product of a desire to join the city's two existing school districts, evoked these feelings and something more.

Opened in the autumn of 1856, it was the loveliest public building in town, the costliest school of its kind in the state, and an excellent place to prepare for the university. Seven of its first eleven graduates (1860) matriculated at the university, a proportion sustained as the school grew.

But Ann Arbor High School, as it was soon renamed, was more than a collectivity of students and teachers. As the only public secondary school for the city, it bound the community together, and old as well as young often had occasion to gather in its seven-hundred-seat assembly hall. The school also attracted students from other parts of the state and beyond, many of whom would go on to the university. Sometimes it admitted students who came to Ann Arbor planning to attend the university but found their preparation inadequate. One such was Charles Guiteau, who attended classes in the winter of 1859-1860. He then left Ann Arbor for a religious community, following which he led a vagabond life that climaxed on July 2, 1881, when he shot and mortally wounded President James Garfield.

While in Ann Arbor Guiteau lived alone but took many of his evening meals at the home of his uncle, W. S. Maynard. The early promoters of the Union School had hoped that the families of "foreign scholars" would accompany their children and either rent or purchase a home, "which in either case will enhance the value of real estate in the city." Others envisioned an even wider area of prosperity, since the school district boundaries extended beyond those of the city. Anecdotal evidence suggests that some families did move to Ann Arbor to take advantage of its schools, but it is unlikely that their numbers account for the building boom that occurred in the years before the Civil War. In September of 1858 W. S. Maynard took the editor of the *Local News and Advertiser* for a tour of the city so as to point out the amount of new construction. In all, 108 buildings varying in cost from $300 to $6,000, for a total capital outlay of $130,000, had been finished, begun, or would be finished within a twelve-month period. Unfortunately, the kinds of structures were not enumerated, but the editor's summary comment on the boom suggests a preponderance of domestic buildings: "People are beginning to see that our city is the most desirable place in all the West for residences, as well as business." A year later another tour found that in the preceding six months alone eighty-five buildings had been under construction, and many of them finished.

Even though the coming of the Union School did not have a major impact on the town's economy, its arrival did confirm in the minds of some citizens that "either we must flourish as a seat of education or we must altogether cease to flourish." The man who spoke those words in July of 1858, Henry Simmons Frieze, was no disinterested prophet; besides teaching Latin at the university, he sat on the local school board. Frieze was not alone in his opinion. Merchants were already pitching their wares to students, who as they began living and spending with the townspeople became more integrated into their lives.

Other signs of prosperity and progress were also visible. By order of the council, plank walks were being laid down "in almost every direction" and plank roads to nearby communities were being discussed. Windows were gradually replacing brick fronts on stores, none more attractive than Jacob Hangsterfer's building on Main Street, completed in 1860. A regular hack service began operating from the depot in 1859, indicating a daily rail traffic of some volume. And in August of 1858 gas lighting made its debut, offering an entirely new perspective on the familiar. "Our city," commented one newspaper, "took on a most brilliant and magnificent appearance."

There was also a new cemetery, Forest Hill, which was consecrated in May of 1859. A huge procession, "stretching from the university grounds to the courthouse square," marched out to the site, then far from the regular traffic of the town, with bands, fire companies, fraternal organizations, students and faculty of the various schools, and ordinary citizens all in attendance. More melancholy an occasion than Washington's Birthday or the Fourth of July celebration, if no less well attended, the consecration provided another opportunity for the citizens to testify to a sense of community achievement.

It also offered them a chance to reflect on how the first generation of community leaders was giving way to a second, to men such as the astute merchant Philip Bach, who was elected mayor in 1858, the first German-born resident to be so honored, and a Republican. Or Oliver Martin, born in New Jersey, a merchant and manufacturer who lacked Bach's acumen and charm, but who proved to be a vigorous local marshal and a popular mayor. Or Massachusetts native George D. Hill, whose Opera House, opened in 1871, offered new possibilities in city culture, and whose wealth and civic spirit always drew him to the forefront of community activities. Except for its children, Ann Arbor remained a city of immigrants, men and women drawn for a variety of reasons to a town that prided itself still as unsurpassed "by any inland town in the West" for its "location, physical advantages, scenery, and moral and physical salubrity," not to mention its schools.

Such booster sentiments could have been found in the newspapers of a dozen midwestern towns on the eve of the Civil War. How believable the claims were depended less on the actual setting and circumstances than on the willingness to believe of those who made them. And in Ann Arbor, whose residents "were much pleased with themselves, their city, its situation, and their way of life," according to one visitor, there were many people ready to believe. Those who were not were naturally less often heard from. They went about the ordinary business of their lives without thought of how special was the place they lived in. They grumbled about the conditions of the streets, the lack of an adequate water supply, or the increasing rowdyism in the town, and if better opportunities beckoned, they left, like former mayor George Sedgwick in 1853, who headed for Chicago, and Jacob Weil in 1860. Both men may have suspected that a city proud of its "moral and physical salubrity," and ready to define its future in terms of its schools, might eventually not provide the best climate and circumstances for business. And the census of 1860, with its disclosure that Ann Arbor was no longer Michigan's second city in wealth and population, would have fed that suspicion.

But concern over the city's business future would soon give way to fears about the fate of the Union. In the presidential election of 1860 Abraham Lincoln won Ann Arbor by ninety-one votes, thanks to the overwhelmingly Republican vote in the First Ward, the city's largest and wealthiest. What had once been a Whig majority now translated into a Republican, as anti-slavery, anti-drink, anti-alien, and anti-Catholic feelings rallied around the flag of the new, Michigan-born party. The shift was true in state as well as national elections, and even in local races, where personal attachments played a larger role, Republicans held an edge estimated at sixty to seventy-five votes. Democratic candidates fared well in ward races, especially in the second (German) and the fourth (Irish), but the mayor's chair was a difficult prize: W. S. Maynard had won by a single vote in 1856. The Germans, moreover, complicated the political calculus, for when a Philip Bach or, later (1868), a Christian Eberbach ran for mayor under the Republican banner, the German vote tended to follow, leaving Democrats complaining about "nationality" outweighing party.

Soon after the 1860 election the citizens were caught up in the anxieties affecting the rest of the country as secessionist rhetoric evolved into political fact. Newspapers regularly ran articles marking the progress of the national crisis, and at their January 1861 meeting the Steuben Guards, a local military company organized in 1859 and comprised largely of German immigrants, resolved to offer its "services . . . to the Commander-in-Chief of the forces of the State, and to assure him . . . of our readiness and desire to defend and vindicate . . . the laws and constitution of our adopted country." Students at the university were also girding themselves for battle by devoting spare hours to military drill and voicing their patriotism with displays of the flag. News of the attack on Fort Sumter and its subsequent surrender finally snapped the months of tension, and on the afternoon of April 15, 1861, the citizens of Ann Arbor did what they had always done in moments of crisis—they gathered at the courthouse.

There they selected Dr. Tappan to preside over the meeting—evidence of his standing in the community—and listened as he and other prominent townspeople spoke to their concerns. Ultimately they passed resolutions to support Lincoln and to set up a committee to assist in organizing the military companies the president was expected to ask for. In the weeks that followed, the citizens enveloped themselves in the patriotic enthusiasm so common to the beginning of wars. They cheered as the Steuben Guard contingent of seventy-five men left to rendezvous at Fort Wayne with the rest of the First Michigan Regiment. They contributed individually to Governor Austin Blair's request for a $100,000 loan to the state. They voted to tax themselves $5,000 to support "the families of those husbands and fathers who have gone into the service of their country." And they listened to speeches and sermons by the hour. Men from sixteen to sixty joined the various local military companies, and at the county fairgrounds on the eastern edge of the city, the newly organized Barry Guards went through daily drill, hoping to get a place in a regiment. Meanwhile, school-age boys ran up and down the streets playing soldier, as ignorant as their elders of what the costs of war would be.

The bills were not long in coming. On the night of August 2 the Steuben Guards arrived home by train, minus four of their number who had disappeared in the smoke and confusion of Bull Run, and one youth, George Corselius's son William, who remained in a Georgetown hospital. Their enlistment period over, the Steuben Guards were mustered out and paid off. Many intended to reenlist, however, and William Corselius was among those who did.

In the following months notices of the fallen regularly appeared in the newspapers, sometimes accompanied by stories of parents rushing to the bedsides of the mortally wounded. Such was the case with William and Caroline Loomis, who went to Fortress Monroe in Virginia in May 1862 to look after their son and then brought his remains back to Ann Arbor, the first Civil War burial in the city. Fourteen months later a public meeting was held to decide on how to "extend aid and comfort to our soldiers wounded in the recent battles in Pennsylvania." A committee was appointed to go to Gettysburg, and within twenty-four hours over $1,000 had been raised. What the committee found on its visit was a battlefield "still strewed with fragments of limbs" and a hospital where seventeen of the twenty-four men of the Twenty-Fourth Michigan Infantry had had their wounds treated by amputation. In the decades to come, men missing an arm or a leg—like Preston Rose, a principal in the Rose-Douglas dispute that wracked the university from 1875 to 1881, or Charles H. Manley, elected mayor in 1890—would be a common sight in Ann Arbor and elsewhere. And as they marched in parades honoring the glorious war, they could not have but remembered the day of their maiming.

Less painful were the costs in money. Besides the early loan to the state and the tax to support the families of soldiers, money was periodically raised to coax men to enlist. In the first weeks of the war there had been a surfeit of volunteers, but already in July of 1862, in response to the call for more regiments and the spectre of conscription, the citizens voted to pay a bounty of $1,000—later increased to $1,500—to the first company (about eighty to one hundred men) to be raised in the city. As the reports of battle increasingly filled the newspapers, revealing that war was more than flags and drill, the hesitation to volunteer spread. Faced with this growing reluctance, Congress finally approved a draft in March of 1863, and in the autumn Lincoln issued a call for 300,000 men. Ann Arbor's quota was seventy-nine. To encourage enlistment, the taxpayers, "viva voce," accepted the council's advice to issue bonds so as to be able to offer a bounty of $100 per man. This was in addition to bounties offered by the federal, state, and county governments. Subsequent draft calls found the same willingness to place the city in debt rather than see men forced to serve.

20th MICH. VOLUNTEERS
RALLY
ONCE MORE!

Volunteers wanted to fill the ranks of the 20th Mich.
The record of this Regiment is read in the campaigns of Virginia, Kentucky, Mississippi, and East Tennessee. We appeal to the friends of our Country to again fill the ranks.

TREASON has brought every man within its power to its support; can the LOYAL NORTH do less!
We want men to share the fortunes of war with us for one year, this Regiment having only that time to serve.

The Usual Government Bounties Will Be Paid!

Office at Cook's Hotel.
MAJOR C. B. GRANT Recruiting Officer.
Ann Arbor, August 17th, 1864.

Townspeople were also willing to open their pockets on other occasions, as when they attended a "Festival" at Hangsterfer Hall in December of 1863 "for the benefit of Federal prisoners in or near Richmond," or defrayed the expenses of five senior medical students sent to help with the wounded in the spring of 1864.

To some families the war was an ever-present concern: a son, brother, or husband was never quite out of mind. Even without a loved one serving, the war could preoccupy. It certainly did with the women who gave their time to the Soldier's Aid Society of Ann Arbor, gathering medical supplies and clothing to be sent to the war zone. Indeed, the women seemed to some observers "as zealous in the prosecution of the war as the men," and one, Julia Silk, followed her husband when he went off to battle in 1862.

But most citizens went about the getting and spending of their daily lives much as they had done before. They took their pleasures where they could, their hopes and fears bounded by the demands of work and home. The war was distant, a struggle to be followed in the newspaper and discussed over a glass of beer or after a Sunday sermon, possibly in the company of a soldier home on furlough. *Argus* editor Elihu Pond worried in the autumn of 1864 about the rebel threat to set fire to the "principal cities" in the North on election day, and so urged the city's Home Guards to "be ready for duty—with knapsacks packed." But many of his readers were not so apprehensive, and some probably wondered by what standard Ann Arbor could be termed a "principal" city. Certainly not in population or industry or commerce or politics. And if the Confederacy had wanted to raze a Northern college town, their troops scarcely needed to come so far. But an inflated sense of the town's importance was already an article of faith.

Readers of the *Argus* might have recalled that earlier in the year Pond had brooded that "it might be as well for the people of Ann Arbor to set fire" to the university as to suffer the ongoing criticism of it in the wake of President Tappan's sudden dismissal by the regents in June of 1863. Tappan's removal came after years of conflict over policies and appointments—ultimately, therefore, over who was to manage the university, the president or the regents. While many in Ann Arbor were aware of tensions within the university, the decision to sack such an august figure shocked the community. Tappan was valued for giving life and purpose to an institution that had been, according to the *Argus*, in a "languishing condition" before his coming. How well the average citizen fathomed Tappan's pedagogical aims may be questioned, but only the willfully blind could deny that expansion—the key to his dream of greatness—opened many doors to prosperity.

Of course some townspeople, like some faculty, were not unhappy to see Tappan depart. Like most people gripped by a cause, he easily bruised feelings and did not suffer criticism gladly; moreover, his religious broad-mindedness and tolerance for moderate social drinking had irritated those with more austere standards. Still, Tappan had become an immensely popular figure among the citizens, not to mention the students. Thus the indignation with which his firing was met: the marches, the meetings, the editorials, the burning in effigy of regents, and the attempts to have him reinstated. Alumni too were heard from, including a group convened at

Union headquarters before Vicksburg.

Throughout the summer of 1863 and into the fall the protest over Tappan's dismissal continued, so that when Erastus O. Haven arrived in Ann Arbor to take up the presidency, he received, as described in his autobiography, a sour welcome. "Many of the citizens would not even greet me personally. It was soon rumored that I was intemperate, and all kinds of slander were hinted at." Quickly sizing up the situation while ignoring the rebuff to his own dignity, Haven responded with a shrewd warning. "I took occasion . . . to hint to the respectable citizens who were interested in business prosperity, that it would be well to secure harmony and stability if they wished their city to prosper; . . . and that unless present difficulties were controlled they would have anarchy."

Such a warning did not fail, especially as Haven continued the policies of his predecessor, policies that helped keep "property . . . changing hands so rapidly that it will trouble the assessor to keep track of the ownership." Policies that also sustained a high demand for housing. "Will not some of our land holders," pleaded the *Argus* in July of 1865, "confer a favor both upon themselves and the city by erecting dwellings on their vacant lots? With proper effort made to accommodate strangers seeking homes in our midst, our population may be doubled in three years."

Hyperbole aside, Ann Arbor's population grew almost 50 percent during the 1860s, from a little over 5,000 to almost 7,400, partly through the influx of new people, including almost a doubling of German immigrants, and partly through the incorporation of Lower Town as the Fifth Ward of the city in 1861. Moreover, since the census was taken while the university was still in session, most of the students were counted among the city's inhabitants. This had no small impact on the figures. Enrollments during the war years rose dramatically, from 652 in 1862–1863 to 871 (1863–1864) and 963 (1864–1865), indicating that school was a socially acceptable alternative to military service. The biggest surge of all, however, came in the autumn of 1865 when returning veterans helped push the number of students to 1,205. Michigan was now the largest university in the country.

Though enrollments peaked the next year at 1,255 and subsequently declined a little, the figures explain why students walked the streets looking for a place to live, why some gave up looking and went home, and why the citizens were urged to rent any available space—and at reasonable rates. "There are other Colleges and Universities in the land, and if an illiberal, unaccommodating, or grasping reputation is once gained, the tide of students will turn elsewhere." That reputation was already in place: "I had to pay $3.50 to get my watch fixed," complained a freshman in the autumn of 1865, "so you see how they fleece the students here." But also in place was the excellent reputation of the university, as well as evidence of its integration with the cultural life of the city.

QUEEN ESTHER!

Bradbury's Charming Cantata of

ESTHER;

THE BEAUTIFUL QUEEN,

WILL BE PERFORMED AT THE

PRESBYTERIAN CHURCH

Ann Arbor, for the Benefit of the

LADIES' LIBRARY ASSOCIATION,

Under the Direction of Prof. F. H. PEASE, of the Michigan State Normal School, assisted by 65 Ladies and Gentlemen of this City, on

FRIDAY & SATURDAY EVEN'GS,

November 16th and 17th, 1866.

PERSONATIONS:

AHASUERUS—KING OF PERSIA AND MEDIA,	Capt. E. P. ALLEN.
QUEEN ESTHER,	Miss CLARA BARRY.
QUEEN'S FIRST MAID OF HONOR,	Mrs. D. V. DEAN.
QUEEN'S SECOND MAID OF HONOR,	Miss LUELLA GREEN;
MORDECAI—Esther's Uncle,	E. L. WALTER.
HAMAN—Overseer of the Realm,	ALVIN WILSEY.
ZERESH—Haman's Wife,	Mrs. H. O. HARVEY.
ZERESH'S MAID OF HONOR,	Miss MARY WRIGHT.
PROPHETESS,	Mrs. MARY PARKER.
HIGH PRIEST,	GEO. C. GILLETT
HEGAI,	Prof. C. K. ADAMS
HARBONAH THE MESSENGER,	O. J. CAMPBELL
KING'S CHAMBERLAINS,	H. J. Gardner and Henry Gelston
Magi, or Wise Men of the East,	M. D. Ewell, H. C. Markham, S. R. Winchell, T. H. Johnson, and J. R. Milner
Persian Soldiers,	Charles Richards, J. E. Henriques, and Frank H. Banister
PERSIAN OFFICER,	E. W. WETMORE
PERSIAN LADY OF RANK,	Miss SARAH M. TORREY
READER,	DR. E. O. HAVEN.

Choruses of Persians and of Jews.

Among those who enrolled in the university in 1868 were the first two black students, John Davidson of Pontiac, who left after spending a year in the literary department, and Franklin Hargo of Adrian, who went through the popular two-year law program and received his LL.B. degree. Hargo shows up in the 1870 census along with two hundred and thirty other blacks. In a decade their numbers had more than doubled, evidence that despite occasional racial rows, like the one that occurred on a Sunday afternoon in July of 1864 when some windows were broken and bodies bruised,

Ann Arbor seemed more than ever a good place for blacks to settle. Work as laborers and domestics was available, schools (unlike those of Ypsilanti and Detroit) were not segregated, and many townspeople demonstrated their willingness to treat blacks as fellow citizens, notably the "white folks" who joined in the "festivities" on January 5, 1863, "to celebrate the issue of the [Emancipation] proclamation, and glorify 'Old Abe.' "

The celebrants that day probably included William and Caroline Loomis, grieving still for their son but remembering the times when they had concealed fugitive slaves in their home. Seven years later, when the voters of Michigan barely passed an amendment to the state constitution allowing blacks to vote, the margin in Ann Arbor was more than two to one. The result did not justify the *Courier*'s confidence that "we no longer harbor the old prejudice against color," especially since half the voters did not indicate a choice on a question already made moot by the Fifteenth Amendment. But like the evening school organized in the winter of 1870 to educate black adults who had missed out on an education, it was a gesture that encouraged hope and dignity.

A much greater celebration followed Lee's surrender in April of 1865. Businesses and schools were closed, a parade was held, and the fire companies turned out to demonstrate their "machines." In the evening came the speeches, the music, and a gigantic bonfire. The festivities marked a victory long awaited though dearly paid for: nearly eighty local men dead, half from the Fifth Ward, the least populated in the city. The joy, however, soon turned to gloom with the news of Lincoln's assassination. At least it did for most townspeople; some, perhaps Copperheads or the more numerous Lincoln-hating Democrats, were ready to carry their animosity even to the grave.

$25 Reward!

I will pay the above reward for the

NAME OF THE PERSON

who tore the Crape from the doors of the Post Office during Sunday night.

JOHN I. THOMPSON.

Ann Arbor, April 17, 1865.

Less surreptitious were a university student's repeated expressions of satisfaction at Lincoln's death—expressions that the regents decided should cost him his place. Citizens had another opportunity to celebrate the war's end on July 4, when they put on a huge reception and dinner to honor the returning soldiers. W. S. Maynard, once more serving as mayor, offered the toasts and crowned Julia Silk, the only lady present who had been to the war, "Queen of the occasion."

High spirits were to mark the city for the next several years as prosperity continued to give confidence of a bright future. Newcomers seemed to be arriving almost daily, land was being bought and sold in a flurry, and buildings of all kinds were going up—each now given a street number as the city grew to a size where numbers would have to be used to organize memory.

The transformation of a single block on Main Street symbolizes the changes that were taking place.

The 1862 photograph, taken from directly across the street, indicates that much of Ann Arbor still resembled a frontier town—and one whose economy was still substantially tied to leather. A half-dozen years later, the shanty wood structures supplanted by brick and glass, the viewer beholds a splendid edifice, symbol of a significant place. To be sure, this block of stores was cornered by simpler buildings and fronted by a street sometimes more fit for pigs than pedestrians. But these realities could not undermine the sense of progress and potential inherent in such a temple of commerce. Of education also, for above Philip Bach's store was a business college that had opened its doors in December of 1865. Soon nearly a hundred students, women as well as men, were said to be attending its classes, reinforcing the city's reputation as an educational mecca. The college's advertisements represented Ann Arbor as "an orderly and educational place . . . where expenses are low," a place altogether preferable to large cities where there is "bad discipline and evil associations." These words eloquently expressed many of the citizens' own view of their city.

Glimpsed comparatively with larger cities, Ann Arbor was affordable

43

and wholesome; lived in, it seemed less so. Wartime inflation coupled with an acute shortage of housing had raised what President Haven admitted were already "high prices." And many residents had qualms about how "orderly" the town was. Violent crimes such as rape and murder were rare; one murder victim, though, had been Henry Clay, shot in June of 1857. But arson was assumed (if not proven) in many fires, and robbery was common, especially as the population and prosperity of the city increased in the 1850s and 1860s. Increasing as well was student misbehavior. Before the Civil War, pranks and bad manners periodically reminded townspeople that students intended to have some fun during their college years. Often the devilry was spontaneous; sometimes, as in the disorder that punctuated a junior class exhibition on February 13, 1857, it was invited,

even planned. And on occasion there was violence. In 1856 students who had earlier been tossed out of two of their favorite eating places, both owned by Germans, returned as menacing mobs. Fights broke out, and one student was temporarily held for ransom in what came to be mythologized as the "Dutch War."

But after 1865, with students—many of them veterans—coming in droves, the instances of "intolerable" behavior became more regular. Midnight "howlings" frequently jerked citizens from their beds, while in the spring the city's plank sidewalks—beloved symbol of progress to those who had for years trod in the mud—were torn up as the freshmen celebrated year's end. And in the autumn of 1874 a skirmish developed between police and several hundred students after two of their number were arrested during a freshman-sophomore "rush."

FRIDAY, OCTOBER 16TH, 1874.
TOWN!

SATURDAY, OCTOBER 17TH, 1874.
GOWN!

Student misbehavior was not peculiar to Ann Arbor, but reports of melees in Cambridge or New Haven did not make townspeople more tolerant of what was happening in front of their faces.

Presumed to fuel much of this obstreperous conduct, and other criminal activity, were the intoxicants sold in the city's several dozen saloons, whose doors were open from early in the morning till late at night seven days a week. There one could also usually find a dice game or a billiard table, as well as momentary camaraderie or an occasional brawl. Especially troubling to many residents was the impact of the saloons on Ann Arbor's reputation as an "educational place." Would parents continue to send their sons to the university, would, indeed, "people throughout the state" remain convinced that "this is the most suitable place for the university," if outside its gates awaited some of the "worst enticements" to corruption? Thus questioned President Tappan in April of 1863, while urging a group of citizens at the Methodist Church to "root out the evil influences" which prevailed in the town. "It is not sufficient that Ann Arbor is *no worse* than other towns in Michigan, it should be far better." Neither Tappan nor his audience imagined that the university was about to be pulled out of Ann Arbor; but dismemberment of vital parts like the medical school was expected if public confidence eroded too far. The prosperity of the university and the town depended in no small part on the reputation of the latter.

Four years later there were twice as many students enrolled, several more saloons operating, and another university president, one so ardently committed to temperance that he could inform the Ladies Library Association that Ann Arbor was "disgraced . . . all over the country" as a "place of revelry and intoxication." Though extravagant to our ears, Erastus Haven's charge evidently suited his audience. Shortly afterward he carried his message to the city council chambers, leading a delegation asking for support of the recently enacted state law (March 1867) that forbade selling "ardent spirits" to students.

Tappan's warning and Haven's fulminations had no practical effect. Saloon doors stayed open seven days a week despite a sabbath ordinance, and students went on frequenting them despite the state law. On one occasion the council did order the marshal to "rigidly enforce" the sabbath law; on another, individual saloon keepers themselves ventured to close down on Sunday believing (naively) that their brethren would too. Nothing came of these gestures, and it seemed as if only the law of demand and supply controlled the traffic in alcohol. This situation was deplored by many citizens, especially by local temperance groups, who continued to meet and talk and petition. Over 1,100 signatures, for example, were affixed to a statement presented to the council in June of 1869 that asked for the enforcement of the sabbath liquor laws. And in the spring of 1870 attendance at a series of Saturday evening temperance meetings led the *Courier* to speak of "quite a revival of the temperance interest in this city."

Also stirring was a demand for an "effective" and "permanent" police

46

that would clamp down on the rampant rowdyism, reduce the "alarming-ly frequent burglaries," warn of fires, and enforce the ordinances intended to improve the city and its image. The community had neither the size nor the tensions of a city like Detroit, which had established a police force in the aftermath of a race riot in 1863. But confidence that a part-time marshal and even more part-time constables could keep the peace was crumbling. To ensure order, therefore, the citizens in April of 1871 elected as mayor Silas Douglas, the first university faculty member to be so honored and a man widely respected for his executive talents and uncompromising rectitude.

Douglas clearly understood his mandate. On election night he told a gathering of citizens in front of his home that his was neither a Democratic nor Republican victory, "but a victory in behalf of those good moral influences that should prevail in our University city." Soon the marshal was being sent around to "every place" in the city where liquor was sold—three breweries, five hotels, five drug stores, and thirty-eight saloons, a substantial trade, but far fewer than the eighty-five places said to be dispensing alcohol—warning the proprietors to observe the sabbath ordinance or face prosecution. Knowing that Douglas, the organizer of the city gas works, developer of the university medical department, and long-time vestryman at St. Andrew's Church, was a man of deeds as well as words, the saloonkeepers began closing on Sundays. This success was followed up with an ordinance creating a permanent police force that was to be paid out of the license fees placed on saloons and billiard tables. "These sources of disorder," argued the council committee recommending the ordinance, "may then be made to pay for their own regulation and control."

Stitched within that moral logic is a long thread of city frugality, seen in the 1851 charter provisions limiting taxes and debt, and simultaneously symbolized by the council's decision to use up the pages of its old journal before purchasing a new one. Funds to repair the streets or pay the firemen were readily available, and simple emergencies such as a pest house encountered no opposition. But the city had knowingly lagged behind others in the state "of far less pretension than our own" in the matter of "an efficient police force," and it would be very slow in establishing an adequate water system. Community improvements requiring significant capital were approached cautiously, though not because the citizens were poor, miserly, or lacked a sense of where their interests lay. Quite the opposite. They had been ready enough to issue bonds during the Civil War to avoid a draft, voted on several occasions after the war to help finance a new county courthouse, and continued to give substantial sums to the university: $10,000 for an addition to the medical building in 1865, $3,000 for repairs on the observatory in 1868, and $4,000 for a new hospital in 1875.

These monies, whether raised by bond or direct tax, were regarded as small infusions of capital necessary to sustain the city's "interests," chief of which was the university since its growth so obviously benefited the economy. "Its large income is used in our midst, its students pay largely to the support of our business interests, and while the state at large may feel a great pride in its success and good name, we of Ann Arbor have a special interest in its upbuilding." So wrote Elihu Pond in support of the medical building. Eighteen months later, when discussion over the observatory had begun, Alpheus Felch, former Michigan governor and longtime Ann Arbor resident, told a public meeting that he viewed the "welfare" of the city to be so intimately connected with the university that he was ready and willing "to do anything" to build up the latter. It was, President Haven told the regents in September of 1864, "gratifying to observe the interest of the citizens of Ann Arbor in the University."

The same financial pragmatism determined the thinking of the citizens in 1869, when by a vote of 895 to 10 they agreed to a $100,000 bond issue to support construction of a north-south railroad that would pass through Ann Arbor. A new railroad would provide a powerful stimulus to business and industry; the return on the investment would be considerable and immediate. Could one say the same for a police force, however laudable its purpose?

As things turned out, the north-south railroad was a long time coming, stopping and starting as a project several times before its arrival in 1878. By then signs were numerous that Ann Arbor was not to be a significant industrial or commercial center. The largest industry in town, Weil Brothers, was in the process of leaving in the early 1870s; the recently born Mozart Watch company, expected to employ hundreds, moved to Rock Island, Illinois, in 1871, "simply because our moneyed men would not take hold of it"; the prospect that a large cotton factory employing five hundred to a thousand hands would make Ann Arbor "the Lowell of the West" never materialized, nor did the expectation that the city would become one of the great salt manufacturing towns in the West. "Of manufacturing interests, this city has not really what it should have," admitted the 1872 City Directory, while trying to neutralize this "seeming disparagement" by alluding to the various industries "in its vicinity."

But whistling brightly could not ward off the Panic of 1873 and the subsequent economic downturn. The toll in Ann Arbor was a few small businesses, and a marginal banking concern. A dull economy followed for several years, which prompted the *Ypsilanti Sentinel* in the autumn of 1875 to charge that "if it were not for the University, Ann Arbor would be dead." More painful, however, than a rival city's jibes was the state census of 1874 revealing that since the federal census four years before, the city had lost almost seven hundred people, or nearly 10 percent of its population. After fifty years of growth, the one incontestable index of decline had appeared, an index more worrisome than the town's drop in population rank over twenty years from second to seventh. Ann Arbor's citizenry was also beginning to age, with a noticeably larger proportion of women and men (discounting students) over the age of fifty, and a significantly smaller percentage of children under the age of ten, than had been the case twenty-five years before.

Among those moving away were the Jews, probably sensing that more robust business opportunities and a richer religious life existed in cities like Detroit and Chicago. They left behind a small graveyard mostly populated with children, a synagogue soon converted to a stable, and a rapidly diminishing memory of their role in the town's early development. Individual Jews continued to work and/or live in Ann Arbor, and a few attended the university, but a defined community had gone.

Anxiety that Ann Arbor might "dwindle into a boarding house town" was awakened amidst talk of lost opportunities and the need for new entrepreneurial blood. Leading the way in trying to bolster the town's economy was Elijah Morgan, elderly but still active and still believing in the town's commercial and industrial future. On the other hand, many citizens gladly and proudly accepted Ann Arbor for what it was becoming, a university town. As such it could sustain a substantial body of merchants, despite worries over the growing habit of the affluent to shop in Detroit and even Chicago, a habit that concerned local manufacturers of consumer goods.

It could also support an expanding printing industry, marked by the opening in 1864 of the Chase Steam Printing Plant, and a vigorous building trade supplied by local lumberyards and brick factories. Even as the city's manufacturing sector withered in the early 1870s, numerous new buildings were going up, one of them a saloon, which drew the confession from temperance supporters that "there is no disguising the fact that beer is building some beautiful blocks."

More auspicious was University Hall, whose contractors sought to procure "as much of the materials here as they can, and also to employ resident mechanics to do the work if they can be obtained." And in the middle of the Panic spring of 1873, when businessmen stood outside their stores looking for customers much as farmers scan the horizon for rain, a "mammoth boarding-house" was being erected on State Street. Ann Arbor, many argued, did not have to develop into "a manufacturing place" to have a vital economy; nor did it have to depend on local farmers. It could, and it would—with the assistance of the state—find prosperity in its "educational interests." The legislature had recently (1871) reaffirmed its commitment to the university by appropriating funds to build University Hall.

50

More importantly, they had voted in 1867 to set aside for the university's use one-twentieth of a mill of every state property tax dollar collected. Although a ceiling of $15,000 was placed on the total, a vital precedent had been set.

Educational interests would as well shape Ann Arbor's consciousness. A self-sufficient garden of learning and thought, a "literary city": the vision appealed to many. Ann Arbor was not Berlin, Edinburgh, or Athens—to all of which it had been compared—but a small town in a rural landscape that cherished its arcadian image. A photograph taken in the 1870s wonderfully expresses how the city's identity would emerge.

Sitting in the grass on a spring day reading worthy texts, these students and faculty embodied the centuries-old idea of a community of scholars. Rising behind them is the newly completed University Hall, but it is the verdant setting as much as the academic process that catches the eye of the viewer. Other photographs of the university in this period confirm how the once-barren campus was now, thanks to the efforts of Professor Andrew D. White and the oversight of several stewards, thick with trees and shrubs. Together with the trees that lined the streets they gave to Ann Arbor, in the words of the *New York Daily Graphic* in June of 1878, "an air of beauty seldom seen in places of sudden growth." Townspeople shared this opinion, their pride gradually enlarging as the classes of ageless students passed before their eyes.

The *Daily Graphic* article on Ann Arbor, complete with sketches of the principal buildings, certified the city's reputation as "the seat of a great American university and a beautiful Michigan town." If the manufacturing interests were not what "they might be or should be," the city itself was prosperous and forward-looking. Had not the citizens taxed themselves $20,000 to help pay for the new courthouse, and would not the new railroad draw additional industrial and commercial investments? But there was also an elegiac tone to the article, as it noted that the early settlers, "one by one, are passing away, until now only a few remain."

Those few would serve as pallbearers two months later at the funeral of James Kingsley, one of the last of the giants among the old-timers. For several years he had been living on a farm near Corunna, removed from the city's affairs and too feeble even to deliver a scheduled speech at the great Fourth of July celebration of 1875. In his day, however, as lawyer, legislator, judge, university regent, and mayor, Kingsley had done as much as any man to develop and promote the city's interests. Now six other "honorable pioneers," their ages averaging well above seventy, carried his remains to a grave at Forest Hill, reminding all those present, said the *Courier,* "that they are rapidly traveling to the same bourne." Perhaps doleful thoughts did pass through the minds of the mourners, but as they turned away from Kingsley's grave and walked back into the city they saw all about them a worldly future of uncommon pleasantness.

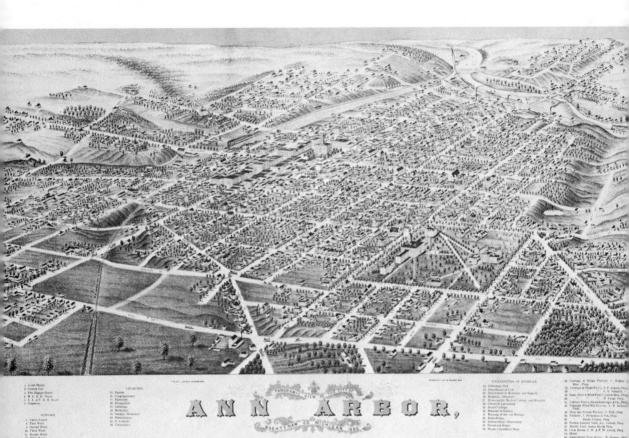

Chapter 3

City of Knowledge
and Homes
1878-1914

I f examined closely, the 1880 "Panoramic View" of Ann Arbor will be
seen to have distortions. Perspective is not adequately limned, while
terrain, except where unoccupied, is flattened out. Such distortions, though, were common to bird's-eye renderings and would not have
bothered prospective purchasers. Nor were they likely to have been dis-
turbed that three trains were violating their actual schedules by converging
simultaneously on the two railroad terminals, or that individuals were
walking in only one place—the grounds of the university.

Such fictionalizing highlights some of the civic accomplishments prized
by the citizens, and the publisher of this image meant to stroke his buyers'
pride. Missing from the legend, though not from the map itself, are a number of industrial concerns; presumably their owners did not choose to pay
the publisher to list them. Missing as well are the city's two black churches;
presumably their presence was not deemed significant.

Represented was "not only every street and alley," exclaimed one local
newspaper, "but every house and building in the city." As a result the
"view" would serve as a "capital *souvenir* of home scenes and
associations." While citizens may once have gazed at this map to locate
their lives, we can look at it to realize how the appearance of Ann Arbor
was being changed. Large open spaces suggest still a place of rural schedules and pursuits, a pastoral vision persisting into the present. Yet it is the

sprawl of man-made structures that commands the eye. By 1880 Ann Arbor was becoming a thickly built community, growing into a recognizably urban landscape.

Even as the drawings for the map were being made, a full quarter of a million dollars was being spent on new buildings. Most were residences, including a fraternity house costing $15,000 and acclaimed as "one of the finest buildings in the city." No local stonemason, bricklayer, or carpenter was idle unless he chose to be. And 1881 saw even more construction, with two new churches, several business establishments, and a $100,000 university library heading the list. Money and manpower were also engaged in building improvements, such as the $5,000 spent on the Opera House. Having passed the economic doldrums of the 1870s, Ann Arbor was "once again," noted the *Courier*, "on the high road to prosperity." Leading the way was the construction industry.

The principal paymaster, directly and indirectly, for much of this construction was the university. It was the university that pressed the legislature for a new library, and it was the university that opened its doors to ever more students, thereby ensuring that not a house in the town was "vacant, and more could be readily rented were they built." This pattern of expanding the physical plant and admitting more students was to continue, for James B. Angell wholeheartedly accepted his predecessors' dreams of a great university. When he arrived in 1871 there were eleven hundred students, thirty-five faculty, and nine buildings, as well as the soon-to-be

completed University Hall. When Angell retired in 1909 there were fifty additional structures (excluding the heating plant, electric light plant, and campus tunnel system), over five thousand students (including summer enrollment) and four hundred faculty and administrative officers, and a campus spilling over its original boundaries.

Buildings were not the only economic benefit the university bestowed upon the town during this period. Students in residence nine months a year had the economic impact of a large and virtually permanent convention. Rich or poor—and an 1887 survey found that at least three-fifths of the students were paying their own way in whole or in part, thus contradicting the impression that the university was "patronized almost wholly by sons and daughters of the rich"—they were an economic boon. They had to eat, sleep, buy books, and at least occasionally spend money to clothe and enjoy themselves—expenditures which averaged $370 per year during most of Angell's presidency. Thus students annually poured into the city economy over $400,000 in the early Angell years and upwards of $2,000,000 by the later. And this does not, of course, include the university's own annual contribution in the form of salaries, fuel costs, and building maintenance, which in the 1870s reached over $100,000 and by 1909 had increased tenfold. Outsiders—not without a hint of envy—asserted that in the slack economy of the 1870s the university had kept Ann Arbor "alive." In the 1880s and beyond, it would do much more, thanks in no small part to steadily increasing mill tax revenues. For Angell not only persuaded the legislature to remove the $15,000 annual ceiling but to increase the university's percentage from one-twentieth to one-sixth (1893), one-fourth (1899), and three-eighths (1907).

57

Evidence of a revived economic climate is also to be found beyond the building boom. The Ann Arbor Agricultural Works on Catherine Street, for example, doubled its employees from fifty in 1870 to 105 in 1881, and John Keck's furniture factory on Fourth Street was expected to do as well. Chronicling this prosperity was the July 4 celebration in 1880, which focused primarily on the town's merchants and manufacturers rather than on patriotic themes. The parade was largely taken up with wagons either advertising the larger retailers or exhibiting Ann Arbor-made products. In the case of the Walker Carriage Works, bystanders got a glimpse of men actually at work as the display moved through the streets, while John Keck, who had planned a similar show using several wagons to demonstrate "a miniature furniture factory in operation," ultimately settled on one huge wagon bearing several dozen of his workmen.

This celebration of commerce reflected a renewal of confidence, a good-bye to the "lethargy" of the 1870s. And yet such hoopla could not entirely bury lingering concerns. Already merchants were worrying about "a certain class of people" who preferred taking their trade to Detroit, "imagining that in no smaller city than Detroit can they satisfy their wants." Local farmers, meanwhile, seemed increasingly inclined to take their goods (and trade) to Ypsilanti. More troubling still was that although Christian Walker and John Keck, as well as many other manufacturers, were now doing well, they were not being joined by new companies. Despite a second railroad and a growing population, Ann Arbor could not attract, or generate within itself, any significant new industry. Some townspeople were glad of this; their Ann Arbor was one of fine residences and cultured society, the "Athens of the West." Others, possibly a majority, hoped for a more robust and variegated economy, an Athens more truly like the original.

To these the federal census of 1880 was not reassuring. While it announced a population of 8,061, up nearly 1,400 from the state census of 1874, so considerable an increase was something of a mirage, created by the addition of almost five hundred students; resident population growth had been less than a thousand. Ann Arbor dropped from seventh to eleventh in the state. A decade later it would drop to seventeenth, indicating how the university's presence, while enhancing reputation and ensuring against depression, constrained growth.

Whatever the city's ranking, women still formed a majority of the population, and one of them, Ellen Morse, was playing a highly visible role in the building boom. By 1880 she had built at least seven "large" houses and "personally superintended" the work. "She is as sharp and close a purchaser as I have to deal with," noted one hardware merchant, "being perfectly conversant with price, style, and quality of goods." Other women were also making names for themselves, and many whose names never appeared in the newspapers—one of which was soon to be run by Emma Bower—contributed to the economic and political life of the town. They housed and fed the students, managed numerous small businesses,

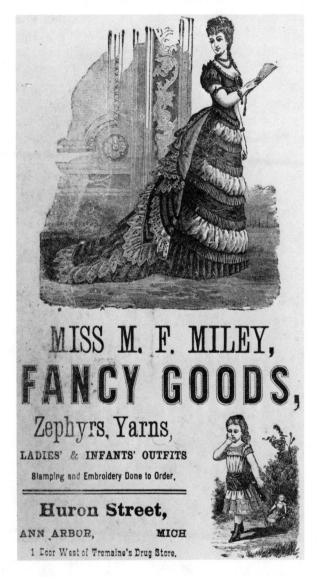

staffed many charitable organizations, and continued in the fight for temperance. They also now voted in school elections if they were taxpayers, and many were. A list published in 1887 reveals that of the people paying $50 or more in taxes nearly 20 percent were women.

In all of these activities women might still be idealized (and scolded) as the "weaker sex," but their numbers and roles were contriving to project, as well as encourage, an unusual degree of selfhood. So too must the sight of the many women who now came to the university. Ten years after Madelon Stockwell enrolled (1870), there were 178 women attending classes—and no longer being hooted at for their oddity. Solid proof that equality of the sexes was something more than talk in Ann Arbor had shown up in the 1874 Michigan elections when 28 percent of the city's males, compared to 22 percent across the rest of the state, had voted for women's suffrage. Ann Arbor and its unique economy no longer pulled tides of immigrants, but to women of all ages and almost all expectations the town offered opportunities. And, in turn, the very presence of a significant majority of women, many serving *in loco parentis*, may have encouraged a greater attention to the proprieties by old and young alike.

But the group with the most dynamic sense of themselves as a community were the Germans, whose numbers, as a result of a post-Civil War wave of immigration, were steadily increasing. They settled principally in the area west of State and south of Huron, and for many of them *Freiheitstrasse* (Liberty Street) had a special meaning.

While still clinging to the customs and language of the old country—including a traditional view of women that led them to decisively reject women's suffrage (179-9)—Germans worked hard to make good in the new. Many did very well, establishing businesses, figuring largely in the building trades, and operating most of the saloons. Like Christian Mack, who began as a "poor boy" clerking for John Maynard and "grew rich as any one can by being industrious and economical," the Germans in Ann Arbor (as elsewhere) enacted the American dream of success. Few wound up wealthy, or even imagined doing so; most of the largest taxpayers in 1887 were Yankees. They and their children dreamed instead of the simple prosperity exemplified by Martin Vogel,

who started as a butcher's apprentice and eventually owned his own shop.

Culturally the Germans were no less visible. By 1880 Ann Arbor had a German newspaper, three German churches, a German Workingman's Association, a German Shooting Club (with its own grounds), a German

Athletic Society (with its own grounds), two German choirs, a German cornet band, and a large German-owned park that was used for German as well as American patriotic and ceremonial occasions. In September of 1870, for example, it had been the scene of a picnic to aid the ''wounded, the widows, and the orphans, made so by the present [Franco-Prussian] war in Europe.'' German was regularly heard on the streets and in the local shops, not to mention at the many German-sponsored social events.

It was also occasionally heard in sermons in St. Thomas Catholic Church, where in 1879 a German-born priest, Father William Fierle, was assigned for the first time, an appointment acknowledging the small but increasing number of German parishioners. Indeed, had German not been regularly heard, it would not so often have served as a source of humor.

But to German immigrant parents, language was no laughing matter, and neither was the inheritance of Schiller and Goethe. Many sent their American-born children to the Bethlehem Evangelical parochial school (the "German School" in the 1880 Panoramic View) to ensure that their roots would hold, and some, like Christian Eberbach, even dispatched their sons to Germany. The 1880 census shows that one out of nine residents was German-born. But that figure hardly measures the presence and influence of the German community, for it does not count those many sons and daughters who grew up speaking the language and valuing the culture of the Fatherland. One of them, Marie Rominger, born in Ann Arbor in 1863, would write a brief and proud history of the German community in 1925—and in German.

Considering that a majority of the population was female, a significant portion spoke German, and a large enclave were students, Ann Arbor was less than a typical midwestern town in the 1880s. Yet the desire not to lag behind other communities in practical improvements established it as being altogether ordinary. Thus in the early 1880s the city obtained electric lights, its first telephones, and finally, in 1885, a water system—put in place by a private company at a cost of only $4,000 (for hydrants) to the taxpayers.

Until 1885 townspeople had depended for their drinking water on wells and cisterns, with the latter also serving the needs of the fire department. Efforts to improve the water supply stretched back before the Civil War, inspired more often by the fear of serious fire—and occasional actual fires, like the ones that consumed the Misses Clark school on Fourth Avenue in 1865, or the city of Chicago in 1871—than by the threat of disease. All of these efforts had foundered, primarily because the taxpayers were unwilling to accept the cost. In 1868 and 1872 they voted down sizable bond issues ($100,000 and $80,000) to finance water works, despite a general feeling, particularly in 1872, that a new system was called for. But differences over whether such a system should be privately or publicly built, and where, in any case, it should draw its water from, regularly divided the community. Moreover, the very scale of the undertaking—"bigger than this city has ever yet gone into"—seemed to justify hesitation. It was one thing to float a $10,000 bond to assist the university or to pay a bounty, projects filling obvious and immediate needs; it was quite another for frugal citizens to contemplate a $100,000 issue to tinker with a water system that already worked. Ironically, complaints about water purity and adequate pressure were to bedevil the new system almost from the start.

Moral improvement also exercised many citizens, and as ever the focus of their concern was alcohol. By the early 1880s Ann Arbor was awash in temperance societies, with nine listed in 1882, including the Juvenile Temperance Union, whose object was "to take the little ones as soon as they are able to understand and enroll them in the temperance army." In Ann Arbor that army numbered in the several hundreds, if we accept the various societies' claims to have anywhere from thirty to three hundred members. And probably we should, for not only was there a sturdy temperance tradition in place, nurtured for a brief period by its own newspaper (*Prohibitionist*), but groups like the WCTU, with its expanding list of social concerns, undoubtedly attracted individuals whose dreams of reform extended beyond closing the saloons. It was the saloons, though, that galvanized the crusading spirit, especially in a community anxious to protect the legions of impressionable youth in its midst. In 1887 the

DRUNK MAKERS

AND THEIR ABETTORS.

Below, says the Lever in an editorial, we give a list of the Ann Arbor drunk makers, forty in number, also a list of the men without whom these drunk-makers could not make drunkards under the laws of Michigan. To say that Ann Arbor has no use for any of these men is to say but half the truth. Ann Arbor would be better off morally, socially, intellectually, and in every other way, if this disgustingly long list of men would every one of them die with the small-pox within the next week. We do not now refer to the liquor sellers alone. We believe that the bondsmen are in every way as guilty as the liquor sellers themselves. We believe in short that they are more despisable, if possible (?), than the saloon men themselves. The saloon men sell liquor for the profit there is in that business. By this means they support their families. But the bondsmen!! Why do they sign the bonds? Can anyone tell?

The relation between saloon men and their bondsmen is the same as the relation existing between the midnight assassin and the man who voluntarily puts the implements of death into his hand.

The case under consideration is a peculiarly provoking one. Ann Arbor is one of the prettiest towns in Michigan. It is the seat of Michigan University, an institution which for the ability of its faculties and the multiplicity and scope of the facilities which it offers to those who seek a thorough education has no superiors on the continent. The fame of this institution has already gone out into all the world, and students by the score are flocking to it from every State in the Union.

But right under the eaves of this institution are thirty-five disgusting saloons, thirty-five *hell-holes;* we can think of no word which more aptly expresses the real character of these places, the influence of which is to ruin the young men, body and soul, who flock to Ann Arbor for an education. One institution intended by a great State to fit young men to act a noble part in life; thirty-five institutions the result of which will inevitably be the destruction of nine out of ten of the young men who come under their influence. One institution founded and maintained by the liberality of the state to make the world better; thirty-five institutions legalized by the same state to make men brutes. Oh! consistency thou art a jewel!

If the Legislature of Michigan cannot afford to submit the constitutional amendment to the people lest one or the other or both of the old political parties will suffer in the outcome, if that Legislature lacks the moral courage to enact a law which will protect the whole people from this terrible scourge it ought at least in justice to the University which is the property and the pride of the state, to put an end to the liquor traffic under the shadow of that institution.

The following resolution was adopted at the State Womans' Christian Temperance Union convention, held in East Saginaw, June 7, 8, 9, 1881:

RESOLVED, That our testimony against the moral corruption of the liquor traffic may be more complete, we recommend that our Unions withhold their patronage from not only unlawful liquor selling in drug stores and hotels, but from all business men who are engaged in the traffic, or consent to be bondsmen for liquor dealers.

Saloon Keepers and Bondsmen.

Michael Steeb, dealer—Michael Weinmann and John Walz, bondsmen.	George Clarken, dealer—W. H. McIntyre and A. A. Terry, bondsmen.
John D. Henrich, dealer—Adam D. Seyler and Leonhard Gruner, bondsmen.	John Goetz, Jr.,—Bernhard Binder and Jacob Laubengayer, bondsmen.
Albrecht Gwinner, dealer—L. Gerstner and Gottlob Luick, bondsmen.	William Frank, dealer—Henry A. Neuhoff and Charles Dietas, bondsmen.
Eugene Osterlin, dealer—Michael Weinman and George Bross, bondsmen.	George Ardner, dealer—John Frey and John Laughlin, bondsmen.

legislature finally allowed a vote on a constitutional amendment prohibiting the manufacture and sale of alcohol. Statewide it lost by a narrow margin (184,305 to 178,470); in Ann Arbor the margin was significantly wider (1,114 to 646), despite the novel efforts of the prohibition forces to win support by serving lunches and coffee "to quench the thirst of the average voter and to thus gain votes."

Why so stunning a defeat? A glance at the names on the list of "Drunk Makers and their Abettors," or at the voter returns from the Second Ward (31 yes, 283 no), provides the answer. Special efforts to win over the Germans were perennially made, with the WCTU, at least on one occasion (1880), bringing in German-speaking lecturers. But cultural habits are not so easily abandoned, and in 1888 a few heads were broken when temperance-minded students sallied into the Second Ward on election day to proselytize for local option among the "Dutchmen."

Prohibition sentiment was strongest in the Sixth Ward—carved in 1867 from the old First Ward—which ran east of State Street and south of Huron. Home for many university faculty (and only a handful of Germans), it usually voted strongly for temperance legislation (166–57 in 1887) and together with the First Ward regularly gave a large bloc of votes to prohibition candidates in local elections during the 1880s. So large, indeed, that more than one Democratic mayor owed his victory to normally Republican voters deciding to put aside party for cause, while Republican gubernatorial candidates, who for decades had taken Ann Arbor for granted, saw the Prohibition Party frequently sabotage their local majorities. "There was only one Democratic ticket," cried the *Ann Arbor Courier* after the spring elections in 1883; "the Republicans had two." Occasionally temperance voters won more than a good conscience: in 1884 the Sixth Ward returned a prohibition candidate to the council. But the most significant victory ever achieved by local temperance forces was not to come until 1902, and was not won at the polls.

In the spring of that year, after hearing several complaints about young men getting drunk in "Doc" Rose's saloon on North State Street and then disturbing the neighborhood, the council passed an ordinance forbidding the sale of alcohol east of Division. A long legal battle ensued over the validity of such an ordinance, with the city successfully appealing to the legislature to pass a similar act, until finally the state supreme court upheld the city. Saloons still flourished in Ann Arbor, but no longer quite "under the eaves" of the university, and so no longer quite as conspicuous a threat to the city's reputation.

Temperance did not exhaust the moral agenda of some townspeople. There was, for example, a Citizens League whose object was to ensure the enforcement of all state and local laws regulating alcohol, "and generally of all police laws within the City of Ann Arbor and vicinity." To this end

66

they published in 1884 a pamphlet containing selections from the relevant ordinances, and in 1885 and 1886 they issued reports of their activities, which included filing complaints against saloonkeepers who stayed open after hours and proprietors of local "bawdy" houses. (More dramatic action against the latter had been taken in October of 1878 when some five hundred students and townspeople, reacting to the suicide of a medical student who had formed a liaison with a prostitute, attacked the "house" where she worked and forced its closure.) Moreover, city officials throughout the 1880s, volubly supported by the newspapers, attempted to control the traffic in beggars and tramps. Their presence violated civic pride; their demeanor seemed to threaten life and property. "In Ann Arbor," wrote the editor of the *Stockbridge Sun*, "it is more of a crime to beg than to steal." The jibe was stoutly denied, and the *Sun* editor, along with several others in the state, was reproved for "picking up every little thing that happens in Ann Arbor."

Sensitivity to outside comment was logical, long-standing, and prudent. As home to a prominent university and high school, the city necessarily received constant attention, much of it favorable. Yet criticism, especially as to its moral character, was also periodically sounded and could not be ignored. It offended the citizens' presumption of being "on a level with any other community as a peaceable, moral, law-abiding community," and it worried those committed to the town's future as an educational center. The city had to be worthy of its role as trustee of the youth "given to our care and keeping during their school and college life," noted Mayor John J. Robison in 1886. If it were not, many of those youth might go elsewhere.

Little wonder, therefore, that the local newspapers regularly testified to the town's virtue. Numbers, if available, were used to support the case, as when the *Register* in 1884 decided that the fact that one-third of the citizens were church members "should put an end to the imputations that Ann Arbor lacks the moral and religious influences desirable at the seat of a great University." Otherwise, simple assertion was employed: "There isn't a more moral, better behaved community in Michigan, if indeed one can be found in the nation, taking into consideration her population." Such newspaper talk convinced few and cultivated the suspicion in many outsiders that the people of Ann Arbor imagined themselves "better" than their neighbors. Perhaps some of them did; or perhaps they assumed that the citizens of a city of schools had to be.

Many citizens, however, were more concerned with expanding Ann Arbor's economy than they were in defending its virtue. Each year contractors and craftsmen did well—improvements totaled $244,000 in 1884,

$300,000 in 1885, and $228,000 in 1886—as did some merchants and most landlords, not to mention those who sold property insurance. But as the town grew, so, it was argued, should its economy, and this required

new and different industries. Self-interest and civic mindedness are nicely married in that advertisement, as they had been a half-century before in the Ann Arbor Land Company handbill summoning settlers to "the most

68

desirable residence in the Great West.'' But it is one thing to invite people and capital to a half-formed settlement with an unfocused identity, and quite another to ask them to a city with a well-defined reputation.

As a place to live and work Ann Arbor was very attractive, but to whom? Were the qualities so often cited as evidence of its superiority those that would encourage manufacturing investment? What had the university in the 1880s to offer a manufacturer, and how would his business prosper by being within a community of tree-lined streets, lovely homes, and inexhaustible sources of intellectual stimulation? As one longtime resident noted, ''the tendency of population and social influence in communities of college life . . . is not favorable to the growth of industries of manual labor.'' Ann Arbor had railroads and waterpower, but so did many other towns looking for industry. Moreover, local salaries and prices were high: teachers, for example, were among the highest paid in the state, while self-described ''common people'' complained bitterly about rents. To be sure, taxes were modest, and the city prided itself on staying out of debt, but these would not have weighed as crucial advantages. By the mid 1880s the growth and reputation of the university had so shaped the economy and values of the town that even those who wished to see more of ''the class'' who ''march to their morning's work carrying tin dinner pails'' underestimated the inertial forces stymying their dream.

Nevertheless the dream of an industrial Ann Arbor persisted, and in the spring of 1886 a group calling itself the Businessman's Association of Ann Arbor was formed to promote existing business interests and attract others. The following year the organization set about to create a $5,000 fund so as to ''boom'' the city as a whole. ''We should not depend wholly upon the University's prosperity. The second, third, and fifth wards of Ann Arbor can never be materially affected by any growth of our educational interests. Their only hope rests in the establishment of manufactories.'' The association persuaded the council to place the matter before the taxpayers, and by a vote of 230 to 78, a small turnout, the tax was passed in a special election. None of it was spent, however, for a group of citizens subsequently filed, and won, an injunction stopping the tax from being collected. Once more ''the element that fights all progress,'' fumed the *Courier*, had triumphed. If they continued to be powerful, Ann Arbor could be expected to ''remain where she is until dry-rot sets in.''

Those who opposed the tax had, naturally, a less gloomy view. For a number of them Ann Arbor was an ''educational center'' and ''never can be a business center.'' For others, including some businessmen, the $5,000 was a no-return investment, a ''boodle fund.'' One opponent slyly suggested that if money was to be raised for development purposes it should come from the real estate owners, the ''chief ones benefited,'' rather than from taxpayers' pockets. Though the Businessman's Association faded from importance after the defeat, it left behind a body of undaunted boosters and a sixty-one-page booklet, *Ann Arbor: Its Resources and Advantages*. Nicely printed and illustrated, it extolled the attractiveness of the city as a place in which to live and work. Ten thousand copies were widely circulated, but like many lures it pleased its creators more than it tempted its audience. And meanwhile creditors had forced the Keck Furniture Company, the city's second largest manufacturing employer, into bankruptcy.

The injunction brought against the booster tax would seem to indicate a vital, even bitter, split between those willing to see the university shape the city's future and those who wished for a more eclectic economy. Obviously a difference in outlook and interests did exist and would continue. But when we recall that even some businessmen opposed the tax, or learn that Henry S. Dean, the president of the association, and Junius Beal, the boom-enthusiast editor of the *Courier*, were both avid supporters of the university and longtime regents, the split seems less dramatic, less deep. And when we consider how comfortably intertwined many of the town's business interests already were with the university, from carpenters to printers to saloonkeepers, the split seems to close even more. Had, in fact, the town been able to gain major industries during the 1880s, far more bitter cleavages would likely have developed, and a far different community.

Industries were one thing, modern conveniences—so long as they did not burden the taxpayer—were quite another. The first telephone exchange went into service in 1881, and the first electric lights were switched on in August of 1884. And like the old gas company and soon to be initiated water company, each of these improvements was put into place by a private company. Loud though the calls for public ownership were, the protests of unwilling taxpayers were louder still. Of course the city, and thus the taxpayers, heavily subsidized the water and electric companies by being the largest user. The city paid $4,000 annually to the water company for the use of the hydrants, and by 1894 it was employing electricity rather than gas to light the streets. Home and office use of these improvements naturally depended on value and cost. By 1891, three-quarters of the residents of Ann Arbor were drinking from the water system, but there were less than 150 telephone subscribers. Only when a rival phone company forced a rate lowering did a large number of citizens invest in what was still widely regarded as something of a toy and certainly a luxury.

With a revived economy and expanded utilities came a new city charter (1889). Over the years there had been frequent amendments to the original (1851) document, notably in 1861 and 1867 when the Fifth and Sixth wards were created, but the changes this time realigned duties and powers.

Under the old charter, power rested with the aldermen; they determined policy and executed it, either by giving direction to the mayor or administering it themselves. Activist mayors like Silas Douglas might persuade the council to do what they wanted, but as little more than an "alderman at large" the mayor had no significant authority. Now, under the leadership of Democrat Samuel W. Beakes, a graduate of the university law department (1883), owner of the *Ann Arbor Argus*, and at twenty-seven the youngest man ever to become mayor, the balance shifted.

Henceforth the mayor was to have veto power over the decisions of the council, citizen boards were to oversee such activities as fire protection and public improvements, and a single assessor was to insure a uniform and equitable tax assessment. These changes curtailed the executive capacities of the aldermen, both citywide and in their own wards—which previously had been their fiefdoms. They also had the potential, Beakes believed, for molding the city into a "compact whole." Of course, as a legislative body under its own president—the mayor no longer sat with them and communicated officially in writing—the council still held the initiative in making policy and still held the purse, hardly insubstantial powers. But now others exercised real power, particularly the citizen boards, which would grow in number and size and confidence in the years to come, thereby making Ann Arbor seem a more truly democratic city.

Following the charter, the citizens got an electric street railway system (1890) and approved a main sanitary sewer (1893). The latter project had been rejected the year before, and still in 1893 a sizable number of taxpayers voted against it and the $30,000 bond required to build it. Sewers might be a symbol of health and progress but so was a city free of debt and a tax rate as low as possible. Frugality was a principle of high importance to most citizens, one to be breached only when an emergency could be felt or a profit counted. By a happy coincidence sewer construction gave work to a number of laborers who might otherwise have been jobless in the depression months of 1893-1894. Overall, the hard times did not directly touch most citizens. A third fewer (110) non-resident pupils attended the high school in 1894, the university lost 119 (4 percent) from the previous year's enrollment, and a third more dollars were distributed from the city poor fund. But these reversals were minor and temporary—university enrollments recovered the following year and poor fund outlays sank—while the city's factories, Mayor Cyrenus Darling proudly noted in the spring of 1894, "have been running on full time."

Street improvements followed sewer work, with the Board of Public Works recommending to the council in January of 1896 that the primary business streets be paved. For decades the city had been "improving" its streets, at great expense and to little effect. No other item in the yearly budget absorbed so much tax money; no other civic topic was as much discussed in the newspapers, on the hustings, and probably in the home; and no other feature of the city so readily dampened civic pride. Still, as eager as the citizens might seem to have been to solve at last a chronic problem, so momentous an undertaking required a careful rationale: "The improved appearance and cleanliness of the streets and the abatement of the nuisances of dust in summer and mud in winter would, we believe, enhance the value of abutting property for business purposes, far beyond the assessment necessary to do the work." Thus shrewdly justified there began a project that would in the next few years cost the city tens of thousands of dollars. And like the sewers, it would employ many workmen.

But a visitor to Ann Arbor in the 1890s would probably not have spent much time looking at sewer lines being dug or brick and asphalt block streets being laid. His eyes would instead have been taken up by the plenitude of new buildings, beginning with the depot, through whose waiting room of watchful travelers he would have passed to enter the town.

If he walked up State Street the visitor would soon have come upon the construction site for the new St. Thomas Church, one of ten churches built between 1880 and 1900. By any external test—church membership, weekly attendance, building programs—Ann Arbor was an observant Christian community and proud of it. The city was proud, too, of its much expanded high school and its ever-increasing number of comfortable, even stately, homes. Seen from within or without they exuded stability and propriety, as did their inhabitants, like Israel and Olivia Hall, or Junius Beal and his family.

And of course any visitor to Ann Arbor would be shown the many new university buildings, among them the homeopathic hospital that the citizens had generously and prudently contributed to, hoping to secure "to the city the maintenance of the Medical Department."

There were other sights for a visitor, sights of less architectural or moral value, but no less revealing of town life. Bicycles, for example, were everywhere—by 1896 seventeen businesses were selling "wheels"—and if not so gallant as a horse, certainly less expensive to buy or care for. Junius Beal used his carriage when traveling with his family, but leaning against the porch of his home was a bicycle for his own use. Nor could a visitor have missed seeing the several dozen saloons, which were by law off limits to students and shut down on the sabbath, but in fact were open daily to all. And if he happened by in the autumn a visitor might enjoy a German Day celebration, gatherings that were the envy of fellow townsmen. "Never have our streets presented such a gala appearance," reported one newspaper on the celebration in 1890, "not even on our own national holiday, which fact ought to be remembered by our citizens, and a little more enthusiasm displayed at such times."

But if the Germans gave color to the town, its rhythm was now firmly set by the university calendar, by the coming and going of 3,000 or more students whose presence or absence was obvious to the eye and ear. For though the city extended its borders in 1891 by annexing pieces of the township, most of the residents still dwelled in a small area, and students represented a commanding proportion of their numbers. The 1890 federal census recorded a population of 9,431, but 2,400 of these were students, most of them not permanent residents. Ten years later the comparable figures were 14,509 and 3,700, which means that even with the growth in the number of permanent residents one person out of four in the town was a university student. A generation before, in 1870, the proportion had been almost one in seven. None of these sets of figures, moreover, takes into account the many young people who arrived each September to attend the high school. No wonder, therefore, the *Courier* could headline a story July 1, 1896, "The Desertion of 3,500 Young People Makes our Streets Assume a Sabbath Air," or that a nurse living in Ann Arbor during the 1890s could note in her diary that the town "always takes a nap while the students are away."

Well it might, for when they were in residence the students continued to periodically strain the townspeople's patience, whether by disorderly behavior in the post office as hundreds assembled to collect their mail, or a "rush" on a circus tent to gain free admission, or merely late night caterwauling (especially on Halloween) after too many beers. When tomfoolery slid into tragedy, community disapproval sharpened to anger. In the autumn of 1890 a mob of about a thousand students began jeering a detachment of the local National Guard company as they marched from a

74

wedding celebration back to the armory. Words were followed by stones, and before the rumpus was over a student lay dead from a blow by a rifle butt. The incident naturally touched off a crossfire of accusations and talk of "hostile feeling between our citizens and the university," but passions abated as it became clear that the soldiers had not been without fault.

A decade later, during the presidential campaign of 1900, student misbehavior marred the appearance of William Jennings Bryan in Ann Arbor. The photograph taken of him standing under an umbrella that warm October afternoon suggests a peaceable political meeting.

But the image deceives, for Bryan never got a chance to deliver his speech. Several hundred students, some of them members of the University Republican Club, began heckling him as soon as he was introduced, leaving the Great Commoner with little retort but a dignified appeal: "I shall be

glad to talk to you if you are willing to listen. I can't talk unless you will."
While the episode was felt to be "a disgrace to the city," it was soon forgotten, much as the obnoxious behavior of a family member might be. For the students lived so closely with the townspeople that they were regarded more like "us" than "them." Their faces, their personalities, their predicaments—all were familiar, and so their shenanigans more readily forgotten. Moreover, some of the same students who had shamed themselves by taunting Bryan had two years before won the hearts of the townspeople as they marched through the streets of Ann Arbor shouting their defiance of Spain.

War fever in Ann Arbor did not climb as high in the spring of 1898 as it had in 1861. Too many people remembered too well that even a just war is murderous. There was widespread indignation over the sinking of the Maine, but it was the students, those who knew only stories of war, who took to the streets on the last Saturday in March armed with weapons ranging from baseball bats to muskets and swords. That evening a mass meeting was held at a fraternity, whence another parade marched to the telegraph office and wired President McKinley that "Two thousand students of the University of Michigan heartily endorse the policy of the administration and tender the service of a regiment in the event of war."

Four weeks later Company A, the local National Guard unit, went off to war to the cheers of a crowd estimated at ten thousand, though not before having their picture taken on the courthouse steps.

Standing in the bright sun, proud and probably a little anxious, these "holiday soldiers," as their commander addressed them, were now to be-

76

come "soldiers in earnest." Or so it seemed, for Company A saw no fighting, reaching Cuba only in February of 1899. Nevertheless, when they arrived back in Ann Arbor in May, with one trooper sporting an enormous green parrot on his shoulder, they were greeted as heroes. The citizens had already raised $3,000 to purchase the armory to give to them as their own, and the council had appropriated $300 to buy medals "as a memento and present."

The medals were presumably also intended for the local men who had served with other units in the war. In all, some 170 went from Ann Arbor to Cuba, Puerto Rico, and the Philippines—not including the several hundred past and present university students—and their casualties were slight. One died of disease, another lost a leg in Cuba, and a third had his jaw shot away in Manila. No Gettysburg, this brief Gilbert and Sullivan war, only encampments, marches, and souvenirs to inspire civic pride. "That they have seen little of actual war is no fault of theirs," editorialized the *Argus*. "They were ready to meet every demand of them and did so meet them."

While attention had been preoccupied with Cuba and the Philippines, Ann Arbor turned seventy-five years old. No public celebration was held, though elderly inhabitants like Christian Eberbach, still active in his pharmaceutical business, and Maria Hiscock, the mayor's mother, were undoubtedly asked by friends to reminisce about the village they had come to in the 1830s, a small, crude frontier settlement indistinguishable from countless others. Of course, measured by population, commerce, or industry, Ann Arbor was still a small town, one whose businessmen were inclined to view the new interurban connection with Detroit less as a symbol of progress than as yet another means by which "home establishments" would lose trade.

At the same time, however, virtually all of the citizens took pride in what their community had become, a famous university town, one enhanced by its verdant beauty and rich culture. The latter was now embellished with a yearly May Festival and a private school of music whose new home had been built with $15,000 in citizen subscriptions. Long a part of community leisure, music was becoming a staple of the city's economy and identity. No wonder that some residents were ready to believe that the equal of Ann Arbor could not "be found in the broad union." Such rhapsodies were naturally loudest in the town itself, but also could be heard far away; as an important four-year station in life to thousands, or a significant stop for thousands more—or merely a postcard vision for countless others—Ann Arbor was continually creating admirers. To pilgrims and permanent residents alike, the city was at once a place, a home, a retreat, and, for some, a way of life.

AT THE GATES OF MECCA

In the next seventy-five years it would continue to inspire such feelings, despite losing some of the quiet charm its name evoked. And despite being overshadowed by the institution that had made its fortune.

By the turn of the century the university was faced with having to expand its physical plant to accommodate the ever-growing numbers and needs of its students and faculty. Classrooms, laboratories, libraries, hospitals—the old, where feasible, had to be enlarged, and new ones built. A university, in President Angell's words, might be made "out of men and not out of brick and mortar," but even Henry Tappan, passionate advocate of this philosophy, had built an observatory. Angell was to do much more, especially in the later years of his presidency, and his successors did even more.

Reporting to the regents in September of 1903, Angell announced that "never before in the history of the university" had there been so much "construction of new buildings . . . at once." Local newspapers reported the same phenomenon in the same hyperbole, although from a different perspective: "Never before has there been such a demand for labor and never before has skilled labor been so scarce. Every carpenter and mason who is able and willing to work is employed at big wages." The enthusiasm was not misplaced, for the city was in the throes of the busiest building boom of its history, and two-thirds of the almost $600,000 spent on construction in 1902 went into the university.

Expansion involved more than brick and mortar. Confined for half a century to its original forty acres plus the four-acre site of the observatory, the university now began to extend its physical boundaries. By gift and purchase it took up properties in all directions, helped out not only by the beneficence of supporters, regents, and alumni—already by 1902 the largest such group in the country—but by a provision of the state constitution of 1908 giving the regents the power of eminent domain. This power was first exercised in 1911 to obtain a lot on Thayer Street needed for the site of Hill Auditorium. The city as well was helpful, purchasing and then deeding to the university in 1899 a plot of land for the new homeopathic hospital and in 1906 turning over twenty-three acres of land for an arboretum.

These parcels were just the beginning. In the years ahead hundreds of acres in the city would come under university control, with streets sometimes being rerouted or closed to satisfy its needs. Questions and complaints were occasionally voiced because lives were interrupted and tax revenues reduced, but the process was inevitable. Students were clamoring to come, and the state was willing to subsidize, steadily raising the mill tax to the level where in the last year of Angell's presidency over a half million dollars was generated. And as the university swelled in space, revenues, and numbers—and extended its calendar to include a summer session already topping one thousand students—so did outsiders increasingly think and speak of *it* as Ann Arbor.

The Angell building program, like those of his successors, offered employment. Much of it was the kind black laborers could readily claim and did. Between 1900 and 1910 the number of blacks living in Ann Arbor jumped by nearly 50 percent, reaching 515, or approximately 3.5 percent of the permanent population. Those not laying bricks or hammering nails on building sites cooked or cut hair for students, washed the clothes and set the tables of the middle class, and drove the carriages of the likes of Regent Junius Beal and President Angell. None as yet taught in the university or argued cases in the courthouse, but on Fuller Street a black physician, Katherine Crawford, tended to their health. Born and raised in Ann Arbor, she received her medical degree from the university in 1898. Besides ministering to the sick, she may well have been urged as an inspiring role model to black children, who learned their letters and daydreamed their futures in the city's schools.

On Sundays these children and their parents were likely to be found in one of the black churches, where dignity was renewed and identity strengthened, and where they did not need to be on guard. For outside home and church, blacks could not avoid hearing or seeing or reading reminders of the terms in which many whites accepted them. Consider how Hugh Johnson, a cafe owner, was described in a 1906 booster pamphlet: "Hugh is a true type of Mississippi chocolate brown with the loyal spirit and firmness of character that is found in the genuine colored race and deserves fully the respect and confidence of the public which he unmistakably holds."

Such patronizing attention, however, did not prevent blacks from asking for what they thought they deserved. In 1901 a group "respectfully petitioned" incoming mayor Royal Copeland to appoint Samuel Wilson, a black man, to the police force. Along with their petition came one from a group of white Republicans also urging the mayor to appoint Wilson, "believing that the colored voters of Ann Arbor, who have always shown themselves loyal to the Republican Party in this city, deserve some recognition by that party." Hard political realities lay behind that appeal. In the preceding fifteen years, city Republicans had seen their majority slipping away, not simply because of the appeal of the Prohibition Party, but because second-generation Germans and Irish, whose birthrates tended to be higher than that of the Yankees, carried on the tradition of voting Democratic. A third petition from another group of blacks asked for the appointment of William Blackburn. Mayor Copeland selected neither candidate, but six years later Blackburn, after serving as an elected constable from the Fifth Ward, was appointed to the police force by another Republican mayor. By then he had ceased being designated "colored" in city directories. A glance at a 1908 photo of the police—resplendent in their new Detroit-made "metropolitan style" uniforms—tells why.

Which is Blackburn? And was it politics, race, or skin tone that finally got him the nod?

Whichever, he and his mates were busy enough, dealing not only with the usual crimes and complaints but with the multitude of strangers who journeyed to the city each year. Special trains delivered crowds of football fans and music lovers, while thousands of others arrived singly or in groups, seeking medical care or merely a view of the far-famed university. More people came annually to Ann Arbor, claimed Mayor John C. Henderson in 1907 while justifying the hiring of additional police, than to any other city of comparable size in the state. And periodically the police had to face students massed for a bit of fun or revenge. In March of 1908 a thousand students besieged and ultimately sacked the Star Theater on Washington Street after several of their number had been booted from the the theater the night before. It took the combined muscle of the police and fire departments, as well as the fatherly admonitions of President Angell— "Gentlemen, this is deplorable. We wish you to follow Dean Hutchins and me home and go to bed"—to quell the disturbance, which left the theater a shambles and the invading host more proud than sorry.

**A Student of the U. of M. "Riot Course"
returning from a recitation.**

The 1910 census, which carefully avoided counting university students in order to give a true profile of the community, listed just under 15,000 permanent residents, an increase of over 3,000 since the 1900 census. Large though it was, the 25 percent increase fell short of what those who measured by brick and mortar had anticipated. "Ann Arbor people," wrote the *Daily Times-News*, "had secured an idea that the city was much larger than it really is because of the great growth in population in the past decade as evidenced by the increase in every line of business and the building operations in particular."

Some of that increase in business had been due to the efforts of the Board of Commerce, which had been organized in February of 1907 and a year later raised $40,000 in subscriptions to be used to secure new "manufacturing interests." No one filed suit about these dollars—a voluntary fund was not a booster tax—and within a year a ladder manufacturing company had become the beneficiary of the first $10,000. But Ann Arbor, with 783 hands employed in sixty-three factories, was still a long way in 1910 from being a blue-collar town. Various attempts to manufacture automobiles in the city failed, and the collapse in 1912 of a plumbing supply company less than two years after the Board of Commerce had tempted it away from New York was embarrassing. Only the establishment in 1913 of the Hoover Steel Ball Company, financed almost entirely by local capital, promised a significant industrial future.

Meanwhile, white-collar and service jobs suitable for women, who now outnumbered men by almost 1,500, continued to expand. Some women worked in the professions; most earned a living by boarding students, nursing the sick, laboring as domestics, and clerking in shops and offices.

They could also be found in factories, but seemed, as we might expect, not to fit the ordinary image. A state factory inspector who had checked Ann Arbor earlier in the decade thought it unlike the "ordinary factory town. The girls are very polite and indicate by their actions and speech that they have good homes and home training."

These were pleasing words to citizens whose pride in their homes equaled their pride in their schools. Indeed, one member of the Board of Commerce, former mayor Samuel Beakes, believed that while the city needed more industry, promoting it as "a residence place" would encourage growth "along the lines of least resistance." No better advertisement for such a campaign could have been found than the 1907 photograph of one branch of the Allmendinger clan gathered *unter dem Baum* near their west side house, a photograph suffused with that sense of stability, decorum, and well-being that a home gave.

A family gathered under a tree, students and faculty gathered in the grass; these are key images in understanding the development of Ann Arbor in the late nineteenth and early twentieth centuries, for they tell us of ideals, which are no less important than facts. What citizens imagined and desired for their community often shaped their response to the challenge of realities. When the high school was destroyed by fire on the last day of 1904, taxpayers—the charred building standing as a violation of their memories—overwhelmingly voted to raise $200,000 in bonds, spread over thirty years, to see it rebuilt.

The sum was extraordinary, but so had been the love for the school, and its importance as a symbol of identity.

A "City of Knowledge and Homes" was the motto adopted by the Ann Arbor Civic Association in 1913, and it was a motto that resonated deeply. Not simply because 85 percent of the permanent residents were said to own their own homes, or that schools were the foundation of the economy, but also because the value and purposes of home and school were thought to be complementary. Home was the primary classroom for teaching values; knowledge was still regarded as including the capacity and responsibility to lead a virtuous life. If nature was regularly thanked for having "done great things for us here," home and knowledge, the work of its citizens, were assumed to embody both the meaning and the future of Ann Arbor.

How that future would develop was the primary concern of the Civic Association, which was born out of a desire to replace the business-oriented boosterism of the Board of Commerce with an organization whose goal would be "real civic advancement." Forty enthusiastic citizens attended its organizational meeting in January of 1913, and within a year membership numbered over four hundred. The belief that citizens working together could substantially improve the conditions of their city had taken hold. It was strengthened by the progressive spirit of the day—in the spring of 1913 the Progressive Party would win three wards in the mayoral race and elect an alderman—and by the gospel that Ann Arbor was a special place. It was strengthened as well by the garbage and manure piles that blighted vacant lots and streets, public lighting that was inadequate in many areas, and houses that were being built without concern for placement. Existing photographs from this era, usually focused on special moments or enduring charms, seldom reveal the less appealing aspects of the physical environment.

The association also set itself to look into the moral environment of the city. Doubtless it was goaded by a campaign announced the year before by the Social Purity Club—a group representing twelve women's organizations. Its goals were to oust "objectionable resorts and public characters," to enforce the laws regarding the sale of alcohol to minors, and to ensure that sex hygiene was taught in both homes and schools. This last objective grew out of a sensational study issued by social worker Agnes Inglis in October of 1911, which claimed that many young women in Ann Arbor lived without "supervision" in rooming houses and that consequently "loathsome diseases" were widespread. How "frightful" the situation actually was is unclear, since Inglis, who in 1916 would open a birth control clinic in Ann Arbor before Margaret Sanger opened hers in New York, was unable to furnish statistics. But a city that depended so much on its reputation could ill afford to ignore reports of immoral and unhealthy conditions.

Efforts were also to be made to improve the town's economy, and within a few months the Committee on Industry and Labor had found new occupants for three plants hitherto "either unoccupied or working in a perfunctory manner." But what individuals like businessman G. F. Allmendinger, the first president of the association, and Mayor William Walz, an ardent supporter, fundamentally wanted was a clean, well-lighted "city of residences," capitalizing on "the things for which our city is adapted." One of the more aggressively run programs was the "anti-fly crusade," which saw hundreds of schoolchildren, instructed by Doctor Dawson's "Catechism on the Fly" and armed with flyswatters, trying to rid the city of "this most deadly of human enemies."

If such campaigns leave us chuckling, the work of the Civic Association as a whole should not. Its efforts to further beautify the city by planting trees and shrubs had real effect, and it was the guiding force behind an attempt to revise the city charter. Perhaps as important as its programs, however, was the spirit in which it worked. "If we cannot succeed in being the first flyless city," wrote those in charge of the fly campaign, "let us be so united in our struggle for the ideal human environment that we may be a 'City with a Conscience.' " At once secular and religious, that reaching for civic virtue was in earnest, and in a city the size and character of Ann Arbor, altogether possible. At least, that is, in the eyes of adults of that period, who had few doubts as to what virtue was, who could remember a bloody civil war for virtue, and who had built churches and schools and civic organizations to instill it.

As we examine their faces today, their confidence and clarity about virtue, be they firemen, merchants, or clubmen, seems written into the matter-of-fact way they look at the camera. Their children would learn to smile at the camera, and their grandchildren would learn to smile at the mention of virtue.

On the first anniversary of the Civic Association a grand banquet was held, with toastmaster Junius Beal telling the assembled members that their success was due to good leadership and citizens "willing and anxious to show how they could make their city a better place to live in." The same note was struck by the guest speaker of the evening, the Reverend Carl Patton, former minister of the Congregational Church, who lauded the "new spirit of progress" that had come to Ann Arbor since he had left in 1911.

While the Civic Association was responsible for lately shaping this spirit, others deserved the credit for many of its works. It had been the townspeople, after years of complaints and rancorous negotiations, who finally voted in May of 1913 to buy out the Water Company and set up a municipal system. It had been the council, three months later, that had prudently voted to give the university $25,000 to build a hospital "for the sole use of patients taken sick of contagious diseases in the city of Ann Arbor." And one man, Professor George P. Burns, had been the catalyst in establishing the Park Commission back in 1905, which in the next five years added almost two hundred acres to city park land. All of these efforts seemed to prove the lesson the Reverend Patton had wanted to draw: that it was "people who have purposes that are steadfast and high [who] will make a great city."

Another great festivity was also held in the spring of 1914. On April 1, several thousand German-Americans crowded into Hill Auditorium to honor the anniversary of the birth of Otto von Bismarck (1815-1898), the famed "Iron Chancellor" of Germany. With pride they heard President Hutchins praise the German community of Michigan for its help in building the university—"none had a greater part"; and they broke out in "great applause" when Hutchins went on to record that 25 percent of the students were of German extraction and that "nearly all" of the faculty had either studied German or studied in Germany. The main speaker of the day was the German consul general of Chicago, who was introduced by Mayor R.G. Mackenzie "speaking excellent German." When it came time for the consul general's address on German economic development since 1871, he spoke in English, a concession to some in the audience, a difficulty for others.

For although English was now regularly heard in the German community—evening services in English were begun at Bethlehem Church in

1909, and the attached school had been bilingual since 1906—the mother tongue was not forsaken, especially by older members. *Die Washtenaw Post* was still published in Ann Arbor, and it had urged its readers to attend the celebration and bring their children ("nicht die Babies"). In this atmosphere of good feeling the *Daily Times-News* chose to speak of Bismarck in the most complimentary terms, as a "frat man" who valued university life, as a friend of the Union during the Civil War, and as the most "American German who ever lived, if to be American is taken as implying the virtues of common sense, the willingness and ability to work hard and to lead a clean life in the service of humanity."

Such praise, and at such a time, was altogether acceptable to residents of a small city with a strongly German heritage and an economy geared to a university directly patterned on the German model. Archduke Franz Ferdinand had not yet been assassinated, and the bickering of statesmen an ocean removed seemed far away indeed. Yet distance was rapidly losing its insulating power, not least because of the automobile. Slow to take hold in Ann Arbor, it developed its own priorities and was soon causing its own kind of problems.

Dust was one, accidents involving life and limb were another. "Speeders are running wild on North Main Street and Huron Street," the council was told in September of 1911, and in response it approved the purchase of a motorcycle so that the police could enforce recently enacted 10 and 15 mph speed limits. By 1914 cars were common, and they were obviously replacing the horse as the standard means of transportation.

Still, as late as the spring of 1914 townspeople strolling by Walker's Livery on Liberty Street might have seen pulling out the beautiful matched white Arabian team used for funerals. The sight would have been uplifting even as it gave pause. And watching the horse-drawn hearse move out toward Forest Hill Cemetery, avoiding the passing automobiles, they would have sensed that the days of such equipages were numbered. But the thought that the fabric of life in their charming town was hardly less threatened than those lovely animals would probably not have crossed their minds.

WALKER'S LIVERY E. LIBERTY ST.
HOPPE PHOTO

Chapter 4
The City Where Commerce and Education Meet

1914-1945

Main Street on a summer day: awnings stretched and umbrellas opened to deflect the sun, a notice on the trolley of a ball game to be played at the fairgrounds over on Wells Street. Looming in the center of the picture and visible from almost anywhere in the city is the tower of the county courthouse, binding symbol of order and community. Though a separate city hall has existed since 1907, the courthouse and its tree-lined grounds remain the civic reference point and a natural gathering place, especially in the heat of summer. On such a day in 1914 came word that the month-long drama of European diplomacy had given way to the guns of war.

Asked by a reporter for his views on the emerging conflict, James B. Angell, who four times during his presidency had taken leave of the university to serve his country as a diplomat, spoke of it as a "most dreadful calamity." But he remained optimistic that the "cost of a world war" would be "so tremendous that before long the international money power will step in and halt it." Few in Ann Arbor would have challenged this expert opinion. Yet the mad act of an obscure resident of the Fifth Ward was more prophetic. On August 16 Nicholas Yuwer, a thirty-five-year-old Galician immigrant who feared he would be taken back to his native land to fight the war, cut his throat with a razor. His act imagined a long war, and it expressed the anxieties, deeper than calculating reason, that diplomacy had been unable to calm.

As a contest between alien forces the war was an extraordinary spectacle, to be followed like sport, and just as safely, in the pages of the *Daily Times-News*. But for many in the city, Germany was not an alien force but a familiar place inhabited by family and friends, a homeland of abiding memories. Thus while a majority of citizens rooted for the allies, many sent their hopes and prayers east of the Rhine, some yearning for victory, others absorbed only in worry over kith and kin. With America officially neutral the different sympathies could coexist without much strain, and the strain was even less as the war brought prosperity.

Ann Arbor was one of thousands of American communities that reaped large benefits from the war. 1915 was "a banner year for business in the city," and 1916 proved to be even better, as war provided the long-sought catalyst for local industry. "Practically every manufacturing plant," chortled the *Times-News*, was enjoying extraordinary prosperity. Economy Baler, a resident since 1881, quadrupled its sales to $300,000, while Hoover Steel Ball more than tripled its capitalization to meet the demand for ball bearings. Hoover also weathered a brief but bitter labor dispute in December of 1916 when 140 women in the inspection department walked out demanding more pay—"Ann Arbor Girls Rebel" ran the headline in the *Detroit Labor News*—and were soon joined by over a hundred of the men. Besides winning a small raise for some of the aggrieved, the strike also suggested that notwithstanding their genteel appearance, local working women might not be so very different from those in "ordinary" factory towns.

The building trades were said also to have fared well, despite statistics indicating a slump. New houses were down from 370 to 230, but many were of a "much better quality and bespeak an even greater expenditure than last year." Nickels Arcade was the most significant commercial structure completed in 1916, in time to appear in a feature-length film on Ann Arbor ("Ann Arbor Days") that was shot in October with the backing of the Civic Association, and in time for its fashionable shops to serve the affluent at Christmas. That holiday season, merchants around the city spoke in awe: "I don't ever remember a Christmas season like this before," one manager exclaimed as he surveyed stock that had never before been "so great or so plentiful" and buyers never before so eager to spend. Automobiles were reported to be in a "goodly number" of Ann Arbor stockings, and so was expensive jewelry.

Most citizens were anticipating less brilliant gifts, however, and many were complaining about the "exorbitant" price of food. Such complaints gave birth to a Housewives League of Ann Arbor, which cooperated with

94

like groups in other cities in boycotting such products as eggs, butter, and turkey. Nevertheless a sense of prosperous well-being was widespread, and on Christmas Day the city celebrated its first Municipal Christmas Program with a tree lighting on the courthouse lawn. As the lights flashed on in the gathering dusk, five thousand onlookers cheered. They were not unmindful of the war that had given them so splendid a Christmas, but neither were they ready to forgo the holiday spirit.

Christmas Day a year later had a very different tone. The nation was at war, and hundreds of Ann Arbor sons were already in uniform. As yet all were in training camps, safe from shells and bullets if not disease, but everyone knew that before long the troop ships would be moving. Throughout the city homes bereft of the "happy voices of our young men" are "desolate and lonely," said Mayor Ernst Wurster, who summoned the citizenry to an "old fashioned Christmas of good cheer and tokens of love." One home, that of Dr. Louis P. Hall and his family, had already lost a son to the war, killed when the ambulance he was driving as a volunteer was blown up on Christmas Eve in 1915. Despite a still booming local economy, the lavish holiday spending of the earlier years was now expected to give way to more modest purchases.

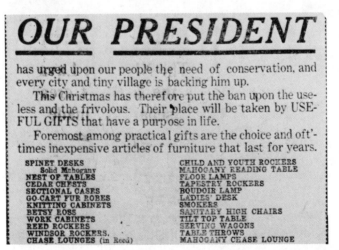

OUR PRESIDENT

has urged upon our people the need of conservation, and every city and tiny village is backing him up.

This Christmas has therefore put the ban upon the useless and the frivolous. Their place will be taken by USEFUL GIFTS that have a purpose in life.

Foremost among practical gifts are the choice and oft'-times inexpensive articles of furniture that last for years.

SPINET DESKS	CHILD AND YOUTH ROCKERS
Solid Mahogany	MAHOGANY READING TABLE
NEST OF TABLES	FLOOR LAMPS
CEDAR CHESTS	TAPESTRY ROCKERS
SECTIONAL CASES	BOUDOIR LAMP
GO-CART FUR ROBES	LADIES' DESK
KNITTING CABINETS	SMOKERS
BETSY ROSS	SANITARY HIGH CHAIRS
WORK CABINETS	TILT TOP TABLE
REED ROCKERS	SERVING WAGONS
WINDSOR ROCKERS.	TABLE THROWS
CHASE LOUNGES (in Reed)	MAHOGANY CHASE LOUNGE

No public tree lighting was held this year; instead, those who had heeded the campaign to join the Red Cross—some 5,600 residents—displayed the organization's flag in lighted windows. Many of those same homes were now without student boarders, for university enrollments had plummeted from 7,500 to 6,000 in the past year, and some homes were without adequate heat as the city suffered through a national coal shortage.

Further unsettling the holiday mood was the realization that not everyone in Ann Arbor supported the national cause. For those who could read

German the editorials in Eugene Helber's *Die Washtenaw Post* sounded almost treasonous, while those who heard Germans speak of the war sometimes detected divided loyalties, or worse. To be sure, the majority of the German community accepted themselves and spoke of themselves as Americans, however firm links to family and friends in Germany might still be. But a significant minority had not been able to break faith with their heritage when Congress declared war on April 6, 1917. If few publicly trumpeted their support for Germany, many more were genuinely torn in their allegiances and said so in words or deeds, usually in a reluctance to purchase war bonds.

How many there were in all is impossible to say. We should probably assume that their numbers were greatest among the elderly, those with plan-

gent memories of Germany. But one surviving clue to their numbers is in a poll taken of the young. In early April of 1918 the new principal of the high school, L.L. Forsythe, asked the students to sign a pledge of "allegiance to my country" which included a promise "to do all in my power to help my country win the war." Of the 550 students enrolled, about 125 failed to sign, some, according to Forsythe, because they were following his advice *not* to sign if they did not have time to participate in the war effort, others because of "indifference or lack of patriotic feeling," and still others owing "to an attitude of disloyalty encouraged by the home." From such possibilities a precise index of pro-German sentiment, let alone ambivalence, cannot be had. But obviously in dozens of households the ties of heritage and memory held, and were assumed by outsiders to be dangerous.

The response to German sympathizers was to shut them up. Eugene Helber was accused of sedition to the U.S. Attorney's office in Detroit and to the Postmaster General in Washington. Called to a hearing in Washington, the frightened editor apologized for his views, pleading that the "war had gotten on his nerves, and that he loved this country." Unmoved, the Postmaster General barred the paper from the mails, leading Helber to turn it over to his son James, who quickly transformed it into an English language paper with an American message: "We feel this is the proper thing to do, for English is the universal language of this country and this country is also our country and our home. . . . We are all Americans, and we will be loyal to our country and our government."

Helber's accuser, Professor William Hobbs, had long been an advocate of military preparedness. Once America entered the war, he became a tireless tracker of sedition as well. Another of his quarries had been Professor Carl Eggert of the university's German department, dismissed by the regents in October of 1917 for his alleged pro-German comments, despite his vigorous denials. Six months later the regents would dismiss four more members of the department, officially because "elections in the department . . . have decreased to such an extent that the material reduction of the present force is necessary." But that explanation, admitted Claud Van Tyne, another faculty patriot and one with good regental connections, was merely "the excuse."

Even those without a public platform had to be wary of what they said. An irate Bay City minister, for example, complained to President Hutchins in May of 1917 that his student daughter had been subjected frequently to comments critical of America and England from her landlady. In response, the woman, who also taught German in the high school, was summoned into the Dean of Women's office and told that her boarding house ("German Cottage") would no longer be suitable for university women.

In such a climate—"You are either for us or against us," warned a speaker at the giant send-off of the city's first draft in September of 1917—witless and nasty measures were to be expected. A German woman was dismissed from rolling bandages with the Red Cross because someone said she was putting ground glass into them. Posses made up of lawyers and secret service agents visited reluctant Liberty Bond purchasers to tell them it was time to choose between being American or German. "Many persons," said one such visitor, "who have been at sea ever since the declaration of war have been helped to find themselves in this manner." And vigilante patriots struck. On the night of April 15, 1918, twenty-four hours after a boisterous bond rally, several businesses and offices were smeared with yellow paint, a gesture intended to identify the owners as pro-German. This "disgraceful episode" was harshly condemned by Mayor Wurster, who called upon the citizens "to exhibit more intelligence and diplomacy in the demonstration of their patriotism." But that was like asking rabid sports fans to lower their voices and clap politely.

Citizen restraint could hardly be expected with the example of clergymen such as the Rev. L.A. Barrett of the Presbyterian Church publicly questioning the religious values of the pastor of Zion Lutheran when the latter refused to cancel Sunday evening services in favor of a Red Cross meeting; or the Rev. Lloyd C. Douglas, pastor of the First Congregational Church (and future author of such best-sellers as *The Robe*), calling for the arrest and detention of German-Americans who did not buy bonds and characterizing Lutheran parochial schools as "little colonies of Germanism"; or the Rev. James A. Charleston of Bethel A.M.E. Church telling a black patriotic association "to oppose German propaganda which is being spread among the colored people of the city." Little wonder, therefore, that a school meeting in September of 1918 carried, "by a vote that was almost a shout, . . . followed by rousing applause," a motion to drop the teaching of German in the seventh and eighth grades.

Institutional records and the daily newspaper make it easier to estimate the intensity of anti-German sentiment than to count the disloyal or ambivalent Germans. They make it clear that Ann Arbor did not escape the perfervid patriotism that infested the country at large. It did not matter that in Ann Arbor, as elsewhere, Germans marched off to war by the score, bought bonds by the hundreds, and picnicked proudly as Americans.

Still they came under suspicion and attack, for the evidence of their Germanness, and thus the evidence of their potential disloyalty, was plain to hear and see. Moreover, to gauge truly the degree of paranoia, one should imagine the kind of private, largely invisible, actions people took. Newspapers and records do not reveal how individuals spied on one another, avoided one another, and sneered at one another. Nor do they reveal when surnames were softened or respelled.

Even as the Germans were seeing decades of respect crumbling, another ethnic group, the Greeks, were beginning to build a life for themselves in Ann Arbor. They came primarily from the same region (Arcadia) in southern Greece, most of them were young, and almost all arrived poor. But work was easily found in wartime Ann Arbor, especially at the rapidly expanding Hoover plant.

1913

1917

During the December 1916 strike numerous Greek workers paraded through the streets of the city protesting low wages, and a later scuffle at a Greek coffee house left one of their number dead and another injured. Many other Greeks worked in restaurants, while the Preketes brothers, who had settled first in Adrian, owned their own. The common dream of this first generation of Greek immigrants was to make money so that they might marry, bring other members of their family to America, and eventually return home themselves to enjoy a long retirement. Some realized this dream perfectly, others a variation on it, as their success—and by 1930 numerous Greeks had done very well, like Angelo Poulos, who owned both the Allenel Hotel and the Michigan Theater—persuaded them to stay.

In their early years in Ann Arbor, however, the Greeks had to withstand the backwash of suspicion and prejudice rolling over many central and east European immigrant colonies of that period. Young Tony Preketes heard himself derided at school as "Greek boy, Greek boy," and during the Hoover strike plant officials together with the *Times-News*—whose manager was a major stockholder in the company—tried to make it seem as if the majority of the male troublemakers were "foreigners." Still, by 1920 there were 130 Greeks living in Ann Arbor, probably a tenfold increase since 1910, when the census did not yet list them separately. And though some were day laborers living in rooming houses and wondering if their particular dreams would ever materialize, more were carving out a comfortable niche in the town's economy.

One part of that economy, however, had recently been closed to everyone. On April 21, 1918, the bartenders and brewery workers of Ann Arbor held a farewell banquet. Statewide prohibition, mandated by a large majority in the November 1916 elections, was due to go into effect in ten days. Gathered, ironically, in front of notices suggesting possible future

employment, they were, as a group, about to dissolve. Yet some of these men may have been less unhappy than their faces seem. For Ann Arbor and Washtenaw County, contrary to their usual voting behavior, had gone dry by a substantial majority in the 1916 election. Even the city's Second Ward, long a bastion of opposition to temperance, had voted wet by less than two to one. Won at last, in the eyes of many residents, was a glorious moral victory, and none too soon considering the city's record number of arrests for public drunkenness in 1916. Only time would tell how meaningful or enduring the victory would be.

Also close to being won in the spring of 1918 was the war in Europe. American forces were now in France in large numbers, and their weight and spirit in the aftermath of an unsuccessful German offensive promised ultimate victory. As spring turned into summer the *Times-News* closely followed events along the western front, headlining allied successes and urging those at home to be worthy of their boys far away. Most of those boys eventually came home to honor and applause, missing perhaps an arm or leg, and sometimes the very texture of their spirit. Others did not come at all or, like Ernest Graf, were disinterred from military cemeteries and borne home years later so that families might finally say goodbye among familiar surroundings, in Graf's case Zion Lutheran Church.

Yet the extraordinary festivities that broke out when news of the armistice reached Ann Arbor—festivities of Mardi Gras proportions—celebrated more than the end of danger to hometown recruits. Suddenly ended too was a year and a half of divisive tensions and occasional hardships, all explained and justified by the sight of the university transformed into a military encampment.

Ann Arbor had prospered from the war and lost few of its sons; the countywide death total was only 65. But the recent influenza outbreak that left over a hundred dead in the city had underlined how heavy the burden of the home front had been. In the early morning hours of November 11, therefore, as newsboys screamed their extras and sextons gleefully pulled on bell ropes and Mayor Wurster drove through the town on the fire engine clanging the good news on a huge triangle, it was as if the citizens were being awakened from a long bad dream. And as they marched about the city that day in impromptu parades, deafened by fireworks and drenched in confetti, they were eager that their lives and their town should resume familiar patterns.

They would, except that prewar patterns would not hold. The students returned, but in unprecedented numbers (8,500 in 1919, over 9,600 in 1920), contributing to a worse housing shortage than had occurred after

THE DAILY TIMES NEWS, ANN ARBOR, MICH

500 NEW HOUSES ARE NEEDED

In Ann Arbor at Once to Supply the Demand For Desirable Residences

Shortage of Houses Is a Serious Problem That Must Have Immediate Attention If Interests of City Are to Be Protected

Those who doubt this statement need only make the rounds of the real estate offices. Let them try and find a house in anything like a desirable location and at all modern and they will find they have undertaken a matter difficult to accomplish. This condition is not at all temporary. On an average of 600 houses a year were erected until the last year or two. These never remained vacant. Generally were leased before they were finished and in many cases even before work of erection was commenced. The demand is greater now than it has been for several years past and only a very few houses are now being erected.

Suspension of building operations may have been all right during the war, but now that the nation has come back to a peace basis again business should go on as usual. In our own particular city conditions requiring many houses demand that they must be built, if the progress of the city is not to be retarded.

The University of Michigan will open this Fall by an enrollment larger by many hundreds than it has ever before been. Those who are close to the situation predict that the enrollment will reach nearly if not quite 9,000 students. Taking the situation from this standpoint alone it can be seen readily that more houses are needed.

Every day or two our Chamber of Commerce receives inquiries from industries that are seeking locations. One of the questions always asked is about available houses. This is a question of importance with them as they cannot bring men here with families and not be able to secure homes for them.

This is to be the banner year for Ann Arbor. One of the noticeable features for the year and an indication as to it being really a prosperous year should be the number of new houses that were built during 1919.

The time to start providing the new houses needed in this city is right now.

The City Must Have New Houses---They Can Be Built Now as Cheaply as You Will Be Able to Build for Several Years to Come---Prices of Labor and of Materials Will Not Decrease for Years If They Ever Do---Help Ann Arbor Grow---Build Now---Every House Helps

Published in the Interests of a Greater Ann Arbor
By Interested Citizens

the Civil War. And even though the city's permanent population had itself grown in the preceding decade from 14,000 to 19,000, every third person walking the streets was now a student, a proportion never reached before, and every fourth student was a woman, also a record. For years the townspeople had more or less willingly organized their lives to accommodate and benefit from the university; now the waves of students threatened to swamp the town and its facilities.

Then there was Ann Arbor's new industrial muscle. With the wartime boom stacking huge profits and enticing new companies, Ann Arbor now led all Michigan cities of its size in industrial growth. In 1914 the value of products manufactured in the city was $2,603,000; in 1919 it was $9,794,000. In the same period the number of blue-collar wage earners doubled, from 842 to 1,612, primarily due to the growth of Hoover Steel Ball. Compared to Detroit, Grand Rapids, or Flint, Ann Arbor still had a negligible industrial base, and before the Hoover strike it had witnessed only scattered and minor episodes of labor unrest. Now, however, the factory worker was a common sight, and if some expected him to be a source of trouble, others portrayed him as a civic benefit, as someone who would spend his wages in the town rather than go to Detroit or "send mail orders to the largest department stores in Chicago or elsewhere." At least such had been the claim of the Friends of Labor ever since the first local celebration of Labor Day in 1901. The war years had seemed to bear out that claim, and so had 1919, the year in which "more money was spent than in any one year in the history of the city, and more money was saved." Prosperity has no better definition.

Participating in this prosperity while seeking a more public role in the city's future was the black community. Their numbers increased by only seventy-five between 1910 and 1920, but there are copious signs of their burgeoning self-esteem as a group. They watched their own sons march off to war, developed their own patriotic and war relief organizations (Afro-American Liberty Club, Women of the Republic), and in December of 1918 proudly celebrated the return of their own. Separate though much of their activity was, it had been more than clerical pride that pushed the Rev. James A. Charleston to protest publicly the exclusion of his church from the giant Red Cross meeting in December of 1917. And in the same year there appeared the first issue of the *Ann Arbor Negro Year Book*, dedicated to providing "a record that will serve as a reference book of the endeavors put forth by those who are working for race uplift." The book offered information about black businesses and organizations, together with photographs of the two local black churches and several black homes. In 1918 another edition came out, carrying the announcement of a new venture.

ANNOUNCEMENT

The Michigan Age

PUBLISHED MONTHLY IN THE INTEREST OF NEGRO ADVANCEMENT

❧ Begins its regular publication August 10th, 1918 at Ann Arbor, in response to a demand for a Negro publication that stands for these principles:

Justice and fair play to the Negro.

Good government and no discrimination.

A Democracy which includes all men.

All Men up and no Men down.

❧ If you believe in those principles, if you want to help a movement, an Organ that will fight to the last ditch for justice and fair play. You owe your support to

THE MICHIGAN AGE

The only Negro Monthly in Michigan.

Pay your subscription now and help us.

One Year . $1.00   6 Months . 75c

3 Months . 50c

Do not Miss the First Issue, August 10th

Topics of Unusual Interest to the Negro and Nation

Remit by Express, Postal Order or Check

THE MICHIGAN AGE

ANN ARBOR   ·   ·   MICHIGAN

No copies of *Age*, if it ever appeared, seem to have survived, but its very conception is emblematic of confidence. So too were the advertisements taken out in the *Times-News* by Claude Brown right after the war. Readers surely looked twice when they came upon Brown's smiling black face asking them to visit his new second-hand clothing store; product and price, not person, normally formed ad copy in those days. From pulpit and press, traditional platforms of liberation, blacks in Ann Arbor were reaching out beyond toleration, to an equal place, to a community, said George Wright, the publisher of the *Year Book*, of "All Men Up and No Men Down."

Once the war against the Kaiser was over, the surveillance of the Germans at home also ended, and people went back to seeing their neighbors as people like themselves rather than as aliens. But no longer did the German community of Ann Arbor have the standing or the confidence it once had. Still by far the largest ethnic minority and still a major presence in the city's commerce, it withdrew into itself, its identity intact but commemorated now only within the group. "Only twelve percent" of Ann Arbor is foreign-born, the Chamber of Commerce reassuringly announced in a 1925 brochure, "and of this group nearly one-half is English speaking."

Not for the first (or last) time, therefore, Ann Arbor seemed on the verge of great changes after a major war. That it would remain principally a university town few doubted. But what would be the impact of the expansion of its student population and industrial base, the shifting fortunes of ethnic groups like the Germans and Greeks, and the advancing expectations of not only blacks but women, who now had the vote to give practical effect to their majority status? Some of the answers could only work themselves out in time; others, it was imagined, could be fashioned by intelligent planning. Instrumental to this effort was a report commissioned in 1914 by the Civic Association in conjunction with the university. *Proposed Improvements for Ann Arbor*, drawn up by the prestigious eastern firm of Olmsted Brothers, was delayed until 1922, long after the Civic Association had merged with a revived Chamber of Commerce, and long after the original dream of "a plan by which the city may develop as a city beautiful" had been toned down to a plan for a community "having interests diverse, and therefore sometimes conflicting, to an unusual degree in proportion to its size."

Nevertheless, the report was welcomed, and its 140 pages cogently surveyed the current and future use of the city's physical environment. Much the longest section offered specific suggestions on how the street system could be improved, including new routes "for the heavy traffic between the industrial section of the city and the railroad freight yards," and the extension and realignment of several streets around the university so as to better regulate the "large amount of vehicular as well as passenger traffic." Attention was also paid to parks, playgrounds, and scenic drives, with suggestions as to how to improve current sites and develop others.

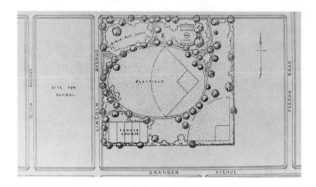

Central to the Olmsted report was a call for a city zoning policy—at the time a new concept—so that the "growing volume of buildings" not choke "the relatively airy, sunshiny and spacious conditions of home life which most of the people of Ann Arbor enjoy today." Such a policy would enable the city to balance university expansion, industrial growth, land development schemes, and residential priorities; otherwise the city would suffer the crowded, chaotic conditions "which so largely prevail in cities of the size toward which Ann Arbor is growing."

Had John Allen been alive to read the Olmsted report and to examine the "General Plan" accompanying it he would have been pleased. As a city planner himself he would have welcomed its inclusive vision of Ann Arbor's future and its hope that the citizens, "with a courageous and optimistic spirit; controlled by . . . common sense," would enact that vision. The record of nearly a century of development suggested that they would. Pride in the city's environment, ambience, and accomplishments was widespread, and it was regularly revitalized by the university's presence. For while many communities imagined themselves blessed by nature and favored by history, the presence of an institution whose very function was purposeful development, and whose members ostensibly lived and worked by a code of self-conscious betterment, served as a summons to improve the physical and moral environment. Of course differences as to *how* the town should improve and *how much* such improvements should cost always intruded, as did "that arch enemy of progress," warned the 1916 report of the Civic Association, "long established habit."

But the interest that greeted the Olmsted findings in 1922 promised at least vigorous discussion. Five successive issues of the *Times-News* de-

106

scribed and quoted at length from the report, and following these the paper ran a series in which local luminaries like the mayor, postmaster, and circuit court judge voiced their concern about such matters as recreational opportunities, the need to support the university, and the tendency to take the city "for granted"—a tendency worrisome to all city planners. One voice, that of a poet visiting at the university for the year on a special fellowship, spoke to more fundamental issues.

"Democracy' is the keynote of happiness for any community," says Robert Frost, poet.

"I was raised in a small town and have lived in villages most of my life, and it is there that one finds a truly sincere spirit of democracy. To feel that you know the other fellow intimately is a fine thought. The get-acquainted idea is not a new one, but it's an ideal one to strive to attain.

"In my home town, the miller was mixed up in every town affair. He was a pillar of the church, councilman and a part of every committee which put civic matters into action. Everyone knew him as 'P. C.' Why not call your neighbor 'Henry' or 'Jake'? We're all in the same boat.

"When a village becomes a town and then a city, it loses a certain amount of that intimacy and feeling of comradeship. The citizen does not recognize the other fellow's status. He is too busy with affairs of his own.

ROBT. FROST.

However out of harmony Robert Frost's ideas were with the others, they were germane to the fast growing city, and in the mind of the paper's editor they obviously fit with the belief that Ann Arbor would be an "even more attractive place to live" were the Olmsted proposals generally followed. Some were, notably the zoning ordinance that passed the council in August of 1923 after eighteen months of study, hearings, and compromise. Many others were ignored, especially several involving the university, which had been given a "Supplementary Report" but whose attention was now focused elsewhere.

By 1922 the university was launched on a building campaign that would change the face of the campus. With student enrollments topping 10,000 and projected to climb much higher, a physical plant scarcely adequate for 5,000 had no alternative but to grow. And grow it did. The legislature appropriated millions of dollars for land and buildings while voting to almost double the university's annual income from the mill tax. The land required was expensive: buyer, sellers, and bystanders learned an economics lesson with multiple meanings. "We first created the unusual land values which now exist about the campus," President Marion L. Burton told the regents, "and then proceed to purchase them [sic]." Attached to the land were obligations to the city, such as reimbursement for the paving on street sections to be closed, which were spelled out in a "Memorandum of Agreement" (June 1922). With the university developing as a city within a city, relations had to be codified. Then came the buildings themselves, among them Angell Hall, the Clements Library, University Hospital, the first portion of the law quadrangle, and a football stadium holding 90,000 spectators, many of them non-university townspeople whose adoption of the football team implicitly bonded them to the school. All of these buildings were on the grand scale, edifices intended to enshrine the significance of their function. And they provided work for battalions of construction workers—whose numbers by decade's end would rival those in all other industries combined.

Naturally the boom created its worriers, like Mayor George E. Lewis, who feared "outside property speculators" buying up city properties and "outside corporations" erecting homes "of the mushroom variety"; or townspeople caught in the path of the encroaching university who would have to vacate homes and livelihoods; or citizens, including some businessmen, who were growing uneasy with the size and consequences of so large an institution. But all these fears of the Comprehensive Building Program, as it was called, were drowned in the general chorus of approval: "It will mean a larger Ann Arbor, and bigger business. Who wouldn't want to live here when that time comes?"

Indeed who wouldn't. For decades Ann Arbor's schools and shaded streets had attracted settlers, some to have their children educated, some to find a role in the university economy, some to relax in retirement, and, increasingly, affluent individuals who worked elsewhere—usually Detroit— but who thanks to the automobile could choose to dwell with their families in a very agreeable community. They did not worry much over the city's cost of living, its shortage of housing, and certainly not its modest tax rate. They had the money to live and build as they chose, and the elegant homes rising out Washtenaw Avenue and in Barton Hills testified to their doing so. They also generally supported Republicans, whose re-emergence as the city's dominant political party would begin in the 1920s.

The affluent were not alone in finding postwar Ann Arbor to their liking. So did many laboring men, especially blacks, whose numbers virtually doubled in the 1920s. What pulled these men was the seemingly endless construction work. For while the university was catching up with its needs so was the city, as it rebuilt or remodeled and modernized every one of its eight grade schools and saw its housing stock increase yearly, with a record number of homes built in 1925. Census figures show that women too were drawn to Ann Arbor, finding many new opportunities in the university as its expansion raised additional layers of bureaucracy. For every seven men working in the city in 1930, there were four women, a proportion found nowhere else in the state. And finally, some new denizens did not even have to move to become residents. In April of 1925 four parcels of township land were annexed by the city following approval by both city and township voters. All told, Ann Arbor gained about 7,500 people in the 1920s, with women outnumbering men by almost 2,000 when the 1930 census revealed a population of nearly 27,000.

Lost in the decade was a role for the horse, long the means and measure of a person's prosperity. The last hansom cabby called it quits in 1924, two years after the council had ordered the hitching posts removed from the Main Street business district. Of course horses were still in use, delivering commodities like milk and carrying into town nearby farmers and their families, but the streets now belonged to the automobile. By 1925 there

were neither blacksmiths in Ann Arbor nor feedbarns, but there were fifteen gas stations, up from only two in 1920. There were also hundreds of private garages, now a part of any new home, twelve motor coaches instead of six electric street cars, and nerve jangling traffic and parking problems.

In all of this Ann Arbor differed little from countless other cities having to adjust to the automobile, although by 1929 the suspicion was afloat that the city of schools and homes had more cars per capita—as it had more telephones—than any other city in the world. If this was true it was not because the citizens had a particular fascination with automobiles or unusual sources of wealth to buy them, but because in their midst lived thousands of young people whose very lives had paralleled the coming of age of the automobile. No generation, it might be argued, loved the automobile more or could purchase one so cheaply. Twenty dollars bought a machine that a student could run around town and hope to stop by pressing the brake pedal.

As the number of cars increased, so did the pressure on the city to pave the streets beyond the downtown and major thoroughfares. So too did the number of accidents. Older residents could recall the risks to bone and flesh of traveling by horse—serious injuries were common and deaths not a rarity—but the automobile was more punishing. City ordinances were made to control traffic, and in 1923 the university tried to persuade students and their parents against the use of cars in Ann Arbor. But a significant therapy was not applied until 1927, when the regents resolved that only in "exceptional and extraordinary cases" could students operate a car. It was a ban through which tunnels were found or dug, but it worked well for many years, eventually even finding favor with many students—not to mention most townspeople, who shuddered when they saw cars overflowing with fun-seeking adolescents careening down their streets. Indeed, the regents' prohibition was aimed at least as much at keeping students away from a rich source of distraction and unruly behavior as it was at relieving the city's traffic congestion or reducing accidents. The automobile did not have the evil reputation of alcohol, but its imagined dangers went far beyond the smash-up.

If the automobile was viewed with ambivalence, so was industry itself. In the autumn of 1925 the Chamber of Commerce, hoping to woo more business to the city, "sent broadcast throughout the land" 15,000 copies of a pamphlet, *Ann Arbor: The City Where Commerce and Education Meet*. Among its many claims was that "Ann Arbor is geographically the automobile centre of the world." What this deceptive phrase meant was that within a fifty-mile radius of the city 80 percent of the world's cars were manufactured.

110

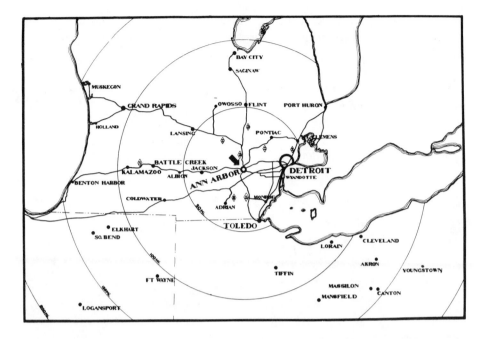

Only a handful of cars were ever actually built in Ann Arbor, and those were assembled before WW I, primarily at the Huron River Manufacturing Company. But the Chamber of Commerce, like a number of citizens, hoped that the "advantageous position of Ann Arbor" would draw more automotive accessory firms like King-Seeley, which made fuel gauges.

Were geographic position the only or even the most important consideration, industrialists might have given Ann Arbor a longer look. But such obvious disadvantages as its high cost of living, its lack of housing, its oddly balanced labor force, and its reputation as a college town had long diminished its chances. There was also the often expressed attitude that only "the right kind of industry," the kind using "the high class good citizen type of laborer" rather than the "ignorant trouble-making class," belonged in Ann Arbor. Responsible for this definition of what kind of industry would be welcomed, even courted, was the doctrine that the city, as Mayor Edward Staebler told the council in 1927, had to provide "a pleasant seat for the university community."

Now decades old, this doctrine had become ever more firmly entrenched as the university expanded and the citizens increasingly lived off its economy. In 1929, for example, the university disbursed almost $7 million in wages and another $750,000 to "Ann Arbor firms or other Ann Arbor interests." By comparison, the city's 88 industrial concerns paid wages of a little over $2 million. Such figures inspired different interpretations: to a cynic Ann Arbor was a company town; to a realist it was reaping

111

the profits of its unique industry, "the industry of education"; to an idealist it was cooperating in making the university "one of the greatest institutions of learning in the world." All, of course, were right, but recent events had made the cynic seem more right.

Even after President Burton's untimely death in 1925, the university building program had gone forward, serving, in places, as a tax-free urban renewal project. The sense of a new city being born, not merely another building going up, is nicely framed in this photograph of the cornerstone-laying ceremony for the Michigan League in March of 1928.

Background as well as foreground commands our attention; we are as aware of what is being replaced as of what is being built. So were contemporaries, and so long as the building program affected only properties and materials it was generally supported. But within a few months of this photo plans for another structure threatened incomes and investments, and thus met with a very different reception.

In the autumn of 1928 the university announced plans to build a dormitory for women. This was not to be another Martha Cook or Helen Newberry—unique facilities constructed for specific purposes—but the first of many in a reversal of the long-standing (Tappan) policy of having students be responsible for their lodgings. The news was met with anger and alarm, for it endangered the investments of hundreds of landlords, the livelihoods of hundreds of domestics, the value of property (and thus tax returns) around the campus, and the trade of merchants along Main Street. Only slightly hyperbolic were newspaper stories of "a citizen army mobilized . . . for war on the University of Michigan after ninety years of friendly . . . relations." Public memory had naturally lost track of earlier skirmishes, but none had involved so many citizens ready for combat. Letters of protest went to the regents; a committee of the common council met with a regental committee to study the effects of dormitories; a petition asking for his intervention and containing over 7,000 signatures was carried to Governor Fred W. Green; and threats were made to take the matter before the legislature—threats that drew an angry response from Ann Arbor's own regent, Junius Beal: "I call it rank disloyalty and I don't see how any real citizen can do it." Many "real" citizens, however, felt that it was the university that was guilty of the original "breach of faith" by perennially encouraging townspeople to invest their money in student housing.

Never before had there been so bitter a dispute between town and university. Faculty dismissals and student misbehavior had irked citizens, even outraged their notions of propriety, but the dormitory plan, said Bertha Muehlig, a prominent businesswoman, jeopardized "the business interests of Ann Arbor." It also suggested to some people that the university had become too big and self-important for Ann Arbor, that it acted without sufficient concern for the community, and that President Clarence Cook Little was "determined to divorce the town from the university." Little, no diplomat, was an ardent advocate of dormitories, so his resignation in January of 1929—stemming from criticism of his handling of several "situations," including " 'local' interests"—relaxed tensions. Even more did the regents' simultaneous expressions of "regret" over the "misunderstanding of the effect of their dormitory plans," and their assurance that subsequent construction "will be so gradual that it is not likely the value of properties now used for student rooming houses will be adversely affected." Soothing phrases work well between members of the same family who have fallen out but who realize how much they need each other. Though temporarily delayed because of financing difficulties, the new dormitory (Mosher-Jordan) was finished without incident by the autumn of 1930. And when a few years later more dormitories went up, the manifest need for additional housing coupled with the urgencies of the Depression made them welcome.

While rallying against the prospect of one building the citizens were taking pride in another—Ann Arbor's first "skyscraper."

THE ANN ARBOR DAILY NEWS

FIRST NATIONAL BANK

Its ten stories did not place it in a league with similar towers rising in Detroit and Chicago, or even make it the highest elevation locally. But seen next to the two- and three-story structures on Main Street, the bank building enlarged perceptions of the city's commerce and encouraged hopes of continuing prosperity. Several efforts were also made in the 1920s to build a large new hotel in the city, which had, according to the Chamber of Commerce, considerably fewer rooms in its "best hotels" than cities of comparable size. All of these efforts failed, including one that called for citizen financing.

"Every Time You Boost Your Town You Boost Yourself"

Ann Arbor's Vision

CHARLOTTESVILLE, VIRGINIA, the home of the University of Virginia, a conservative old town of about 15,000 population financed this $650,000.00 hotel. The Monticello, by community effort. IS ANN ARBOR AS GOOD AS CHARLOTTESVILLE?

Finance Campaign Executive Committee

J. Fiskel, Chairman
, Vice-Chrm.
, Gen'l Sales Mgr.
F. Genss, Treasurer
O. McLeish, Secretary
E. Atwell
R. Ayres
O. Bonisteel
a. J. Brooks
ur E. Crippen
mund E. Day
J. Donally
Claude Drake
Fred Fischer
as. R. Henderson
Roy Holmes
rbert A. Jump
J. Kelly
W. Langford
orge E. Lewis
E. McKinley
ncan W. Myers
hn A. Neelands
ley Osgood
well E. Platt
Jay G. Pray
Paul L. Proud
J. F. Rentschler
Henry E. Riggs
F. E. Royce
E. D. Rundman
S. H. Sandenburgh
Fred Seyfried
Charles A. Sink
Shirley W. Smith
W. P. Staebler
O. J. Tremmel
C. W. Wagner

ROGER W. BABSON says "During the next ten years we shall witness a great municipal race.—a great municipal marathon race. The cities which are now behind will have an opportunity to get into the front ranks; while some of the cities now in the front ranks will drop into lower places. The result of the race will depend upon the VISION of those who direct the affairs of these cities."

Progressive Cities Have Adequate Modern Hotels

It is generally recognized that the city which forges to the front and stays there is the one that provides suitable accommodations for its guests. And not only for its guests but also for its prospective citizens who are drawn to the city by natural attractions and decide to invest and become permanent residents. The citizens of such a city have faith in its future.

We, the citizens and friends of Ann Arbor, believe in our city and have faith in its future. To prove this faith and to show our VISION we must see to it that

Ann Arbor Shall Have A New Modern Hotel

The terms of payment are within reach of all. They are as follows:

10% June 15, 1926	20% February 15, 1927
20% August 15, 1926	20% May 15, 1927
20% November 15, 1926	10% August 15, 1927

The opportunity will soon be given to every citizen and friend of Ann Arbor to help by investing in Hotel Stock. Remember, that the safety of your money will be secured by high value land upon which will be erected a new and modern building and that purchase of hotel stock is not only a safe investment but a civic duty.

Let Our VISION Make Ann Arbor's Hotel Dreams COME TRUE

HELP BOOST! BUY STOCK!

A Chamber of Commerce Community Enterprise

Hotel Campaign Headquarters in Chamber of Commerce Building. Inquiries Welcomed. Telephone 4730.

Less than 10 percent of the needed capital was raised, perhaps because likely investors saw no need and thus no profit in a new hostelry, perhaps because they recalled the many local investment bubbles that had burst. Hoover Steel Ball had made the fortunes of several citizens, but many others had lost heavily in ventures seemingly no less promising.

Moreover, Ann Arbor in the 1920s was not crammed with rich people looking for ways to invest extensive excess capital. For every Walter C. Mack there were hundreds of others who lived comfortably on modest or somewhat more than modest incomes, believing that the costs of living in the city were higher than elsewhere and reluctant to indebt themselves. Public projects whose value to the town's economy or image were demonstrable, such as refitting the schools, had little trouble; projects of

115

mere utility often stumbled, however strongly supported by elected officials. Three times (1927, 1929, 1930) a water improvement bond was defeated before being finally accepted, and a new main sanitation sewer failed once before passage. Both had been termed "urgent necessities" by Mayor Staebler, and their hard passage had persuaded the mayor that less than essential projects like a water softening plant and a city market were distant dreams. Projects, finally, that could show neither profit nor utility simply foundered. In April of 1924, for example, voters handily vetoed a plan to tax themselves $10,000 for a special July Fourth celebration of the city's centennial.

Community thrift was undoubtedly reinforced by a community sense of well-being. Was not Ann Arbor a very special place, a city devoted to education and culture whose residential areas were described as "one great park with winding avenues"? Why then spend hard-earned money improving it? The logic may be loose, but it held for a number of citizens used to believing themselves blessed and hearing themselves blessed. Generally content with their surroundings, they were not easily persuaded that improvements beyond such essential needs as paved streets, now that the automobile was king, were required.

Widespread citizen satisfaction may also be read in the declining use of the franchise—despite women's suffrage. Between 1924 and 1932 less than 30 percent of the electorate, on average, voted in the twenty-four different elections. The average for the April city contests was even lower. Before the First World War the interest in city affairs had been much greater, with voter turnouts of 65 to 75 percent not unusual. Gradually the affairs and conditions of the city were, in fact, being taken "for granted." Ann Arbor was what it was—it had been built and did not need to be remodeled. Thus, for example, the unsuccessful attempt (1913-1921) to write a new charter, with voters twice rejecting proposals and leaving the city with a charter patched, as one alderman remarked, "like Charlie Chaplin's shoes."

Boosters emphasized the city's presence, not its dynamism. Indeed, as the university—"more widely known," announced the 1923 City Directory, "than any American university except Harvard and Yale"—swelled in students, employees, budgets, and architecture, *its* dynamism and *its* future imperceptibly were accepted as the town's. And most citizens were as ready to bask in its glow as they were to live off its dollars, root for its teams, and enjoy the music, theater, and speakers it provided. *Ann Arbor: A Quiet Spot in Touch with the World* had been the title of a booklet issued by the Civic Association in 1913. The 1925 Chamber of Commerce brochure that sought more industry was subtitled *Ann Arbor: The Home of the University of Michigan*. No one seems to have objected when the gala banquet held in

February of 1924 to mark the city's founding took place in the Michigan Union and was presided over by Harry Hutchins, the retired university president. Nor is it likely that any of the 588 guests would have differed with the comment of one pioneer descendant: "Surely Ann Arbor is a wonderful place in which to live; John Allen would be proud if he could see his city today." It was a safe assumption, and one that was reinforced by what the celebrants observed as they wended their way home that night.

No human eye, of course, quite saw State Street as did that camera lens, but the resulting image, as is frequently the case, does record the view of the contemporary imagination.

Satisfaction with things as they were can also be read in the November 1928 elections, when city voters chose Herbert Hoover over Al Smith by a margin of almost four to one. Not a single ward, even the "Irish" Fourth, favored the New York governor. Republican presidential candidates, however, did not need prosperity to win in Ann Arbor. Since the Civil War only Grover Cleveland and Woodrow Wilson (in the three-way 1912 battle) had managed Democratic majorities. Four years later Hoover won again in the city, outdistancing Franklin Roosevelt by 1,800 votes. But this majority was supplied by the business and university wards (1,6, and 7); the other four gave Roosevelt a victory by over 400 votes. Add to these figures the 454 votes cast for the Socialist candidate, Norman Thomas, who had drawn an overflow crowd to a speech earlier in the year, and the effect of three years of economic depression become clear.

Since the growth of the university after the Civil War, Ann Arbor had always been insulated against hard times. University budgets might be trimmed but education went on: students enrolled, teachers taught, landladies rented rooms, and shopkeepers rang up sales, however diminished, not only to residents but to the thousands of visitors who had recourse to the city's hospitals, halls, and playing fields. This pattern held in the

1930s. From the vantage point of Detroit, or for that matter the rest of Michigan, Ann Arbor appeared an oasis in a desert of broken companies and bankrupt farms, and more than a few who had lost jobs elsewhere trekked into the city hoping for work.

But while surviving hard times better than most communities, Ann Arbor was not untouched. Local industries lost orders and, with the exception of the recently established International Radio Corporation, were not paying dividends by 1933; construction tailed off from $7.2 million in 1929 to little over half a million in 1932; retail sales dropped by 50 percent between 1930 and 1933; and bank clearings sank from $54 million in 1929 to $30 million in 1932. Translated into human terms these numbers meant that by the summer of 1931 already 10 percent of the working population, primarily the unskilled and semi-skilled, were unemployed. And if you were black you stood a good chance of being replaced in your job by a white.

Seasonal unemployment was a fact of life to the city. Industries laid off workers for lack of orders or retooling, and construction normally slowed down in the winter. But no one supposed in 1931 that the economic catastrophe that had overtaken the country and was now causing manifest hardship in Ann Arbor was seasonal. Some, like Mayor Staebler, predicted that it would be a "ten year problem." Meanwhile the city tried to cope with unprecedented numbers of needy people, each with a story of hardship, fear, and slowly eroding pride.

Ann Arbor Michigan Dec 4

'30

Mayor Stabler
Kind Sir

I'm sending you this notice stating my case. I'm a resident of Ann Arbor the past 7 years & have walked this town a dozen times looking for work with no success, and I know they are married woman employed where I have been who dosnt need the work as their husbands work, and I'm all discouraged. I lost my husband here in Ann Arbor and got along very well up until the hard times come. I have kept roomers & boarders since but now I have only 2 and I cant keep my expenses up. I'm in debt two hundred dollars, and I'm trying very hard to keep my home although Im a renter. I never see a moments pleasure or enjoyment not even a picture show, every penny I get I must save for expenses. I had a few dollars in the bank but I had use it up. I dont want charity but I would like some kind of lite work 6 or 7 hours a day or most I would like to get out of debt. If I wasnt a hard honest working woman, I wouldnt state my case to you, And all who know me can give you a good recommendation of me, I'm a real home woman. Coarse I dont care to have my name published, but if their is any way you can possibly help me I should shure appriciate it. Trusting you will please do all you can for me Im yours truly

Mrs. Peter Stone

Staebler read dozens of these appeals, and by phone or chance meeting he doubtless heard dozens more. Help was forthcoming, but based as it was on ideas and agencies fashioned to periodic slumps and individual failures, it would not be enough. The Community Fund, the city's principal charity, which normally distributed money to eleven private welfare agencies, now turned most of what it raised over to the Family Welfare Bureau. The number of families requiring assistance, however, soared beyond its resources, so that by the autumn of 1931, despite ad hoc fund-raising measures like a community dance sponsored by university students, the fund was borrowing on its 1932 income. A year earlier, following the lead of Detroit mayor Frank Murphy, Staebler had established a committee on unemployment in order to gain a handle on the city's most pressing problem. Soon a regular bureau was set up to register the unemployed and try to find them work.

Mayor's Unemployment Committee

HEADQUARTERS:
CHAMBER OF COMMERCE BUILDING
Fourth Ave. and Ann St., Ann Arbor
Phone 21931

PUT A MAN TO WORK

Do your bit! Help the Mayor and his Unemployment Committee to create jobs for some of the hundreds out of work in Ann Arbor.

The plan is that every householder who can, will hire a man for two to four hours each week. The odd jobs thus created in each neighborhood will be consolidated so that a group of ten to twenty families will furnish a living for one man supporting a family. This work should be in addition to any other work already being performed by regularly paid workers.

The cost to the individual householder will be small and the good which will be accomplished collectively by our public spirited citizens cannot be over-estimated.

PUT A MAN TO WORK

INDOOR JOBS	OUTDOOR JOBS
Cleaning wall paper	Shoveling snow
Washing windows	
Cleaning bathrooms and kitchens	Cleaning garages
Washing ceilings	Washing cars
Washing or beating carpets	
Cleaning painted walls	Cleaning windows
Cleaning upholstery	Repairing drain spouts
Painting or enameling old furniture	Cleaning out eavetroughs
Cleaning basements	
Tending furnaces	Caring for shrubs, lawns, etc.
Washing	Carrying out ashes
Cleaning and finishing floors	Repairing roofs
Washing dishes	

Please remember, this work should be in addition to any other work already being performed by a paid worker.

The search was bleak. Regular jobs rarely showed up, requests for home maintenance tasks averaged only about eleven per day, and self-starting opportunities were limited. Thus the city itself took to employing the men, and before long they were to be seen cleaning up and improving the parks and playgrounds, planting trees and flowers along roads, and working on a new drain sewer the voters had passed. Paid in scrip redeemable only at a city store and coal yard, they and their families were at least kept from the "verge of hunger." For many, though, there was no work at all, and the city was forced to distribute ever increasing sums for food, clothing, and shelter, as well as operate a dormitory and restaurant for the obviously indigent. All of this cost money—$14,000 a month by 1933—and at a time when tax revenues were shrinking due to declining valuations and delinquent payments. Local government was doing what it could, but as Frank Murphy told his fellow Michigan mayors in May of 1932, "the financial structures of the municipalities . . . are daily weakening."

Many of those out of work in Ann Arbor did not have deep roots (or family) in the city. Among the 155 common laborers registered with the Employment Bureau in January 1931, the average length of residence was 10.8 years, and 123 of them were renters in a city where 85 percent of the residents owned their own homes. A similar pattern showed up among the fifty-five jobless women classified as "housewives," the category in which Mrs. Peter Stone would have fallen. Drawn to the city during the boom construction years of the 1920s, these people had little to protect themselves with once the economy tumbled. And those who had arrived recently—or who were tempted to come by the new law building that was begun in the spring of 1931—could anticipate even less. In June the new mayor, H. Wirt Newkirk, announced that only applicants who were legal residents (six months) of the city could be aided by the Employment Bureau.

Of course many people who never registered with the bureau suffered through difficult times. They were the ones who scratched livelihoods from part-time jobs, moved in with families and friends, and sometimes ate cereal for lunch and dinner. Their numbers can only be surmised. In March of 1933 the chairman of the City Poor Committee stated that there were 2,000 people on the welfare lists and 8,000—a seemingly high extrapolation—"hanging on by a string." However many, they had made their plight known at the polls five months before.

A national solution seemed the only hope. The financial structure of the city was indeed "weakening," squeezed between pressures to reduce the budget (and thereby taxes) and to care for the unemployed. In the summer of 1932 the salaries of all city employees had been cut by 15 percent, while "calamity bonds" to the value of $150,000 were issued to put at least some of the unemployed to work on further sewer construction. Weakening too was the patience of those being assisted. In late March of 1933 two hundred welfare workers, most of them laborers on the sewer, went on strike to

120

protest a recent 15 percent cut in their wages. They also aired their long-standing grievances against being paid in scrip, which, in effect, dictated where and how they could spend their earnings. Four days after the strike began, the council, at a meeting attended by hundreds of citizens, rescinded the pay cut. But it hardly mattered, since the city was near bottom. "City Welfare Funds Emptied" ran the *Daily News* headline of May 13; only cases of "dire necessity" could now receive aid. A month before, in his farewell address to the council, outgoing Mayor Newkirk had spoken of leaving behind "no bridges, buildings, [or] paved streets as his monument," but simply the "knowledge he had done what he could, fairly," for the unemployed. His successor, it was feared, would not have even that to claim.

We know that a happier ending ensued, but in April 1933 people still had little more than words on which to build a better future. Which is why the five Socialist candidates for alderman polled 7.3 percent of the total votes in the spring elections, up from 4 percent in November. Radical solutions to radical problems were now being contemplated by people who a few years earlier would not have described themselves as radical. Even Newkirk, a Republican, was on record as quoting Friedrich Engels to back up his view that the Depression was "largely due to the indifference of great industrialists to the personal welfare of their employees . . . and to the effect of mass production." Equally unpredictable, of course, was that the patrician Roosevelt would initiate radical solutions to the sputtering economy, solutions that would pour millions of dollars into Ann Arbor.

From 1933 to 1940 federal funds made possible new sewer lines, a sewage disposal plant, two new schools and an addition to the high school, the band shell in West Park, and the Farmers' Market.

Hundreds of men were put to work on these and other projects as the city, in the words of Mayor Robert Campbell, sought "every possible benefit which the Federal Government is in a position to offer to the municipalities of this country."

The university was no less hungry, and received $2.5 million for new dormitories and additions to the dental school and hospital. Even more money went to aid students. By 1935-1936 over 1,800 (14 percent of the total) were receiving federal money for school-related jobs, thereby ensuring that enrollments held steady during the hard times. In turn, the money funneled into university construction and student pockets swiftly cycled into the Ann Arbor economy. Such transfusions gradually lowered the city's unemployment rate, which—counting all those fifteen years of age and older—stood at 12.6 percent in January of 1935. That year the long awaited improvement in the other vital signs of economic health began appearing. Bank clearings increased from $22 million to $26 million, the first such increase in five years; building expenditures reached a four-year peak, with a sharp increase in the number of new dwellings; and local industries like King-Seeley and American Broach and Machine began expanding their plants and hiring more workers. At Christmas, store sales approached "pre-depression levels," according to the *Daily News*, and the following year the number of births, which had fallen yearly since 1930, rose by 18 percent—a reversal signifying that people believed good times were returning at last.

They were, and the introduction that year (1936) of the Argus compact camera indicated they would last. Overnight, the brainchild of local businessman C.A. Verschoor became a consumer craze: 30,000 were sold in the first week it was on the market and eventually hundreds of new jobs were created at Verschoor's company, International Research Corporation. The name foreshadowed companies that would emerge in Ann Arbor a generation later, companies that would develop and exploit new technologies and that thereby seemed especially suitable for a university town. But the late 1930s, despite Argus, despite new construction, and despite the grand university centennial, would not equal the golden 1920s, years ever more gilded by memory. In August of 1937 the ten major industries in Ann Arbor employed 2,450 people at an average of forty hours per week; five months later those same companies were employing 900 fewer people and at an average of only thirty-two hours per week. Nationwide the slowdown was worse, but for those going on relief in the city, relative statistics did not matter. The 1940 census revealed that 8 percent of the local labor force was unemployed. Still there was enough substance to the recovery and enough commercial glitter to convince people that the Depression had passed.

There was also legal drink. Once the "driest of the drys," Michigan had been the first state to ratify the repeal of Prohibition, and soon alcohol was to be had in Ann Arbor. Not, however, east of Division; that area was still protected by the 1902 charter amendment despite an attempt in April 1934 to overturn it. Less than 4,000 citizens, slightly under a quarter of those eligible, voted in that election, further evidence of a general apathy about local issues and perhaps about temperance itself.

National elections, though, continued to bring out large numbers of voters—over 12,000 in 1936. In that year the working class wards once again chose Roosevelt, but the city as a whole went Republican, most emphatically in the gubernatorial race, where Frank Murphy lost by 2,000 votes. (The following year Murphy, as governor, and Republican Mayor Walter C. Sadler would work together to bring a peaceful end to a sit-down strike at American Broach and Machine.) In 1940 only the Fifth (and still the smallest) Ward gave Roosevelt a majority, and only 88 Ann Arbor voters stayed in step with Norman Thomas. Five weeks before the election Wendell Willkie had made a whistle stop in Ann Arbor, and before thousands thronging the train station he excoriated the president for leading the country to the verge of bankruptcy and leaving it without a friend in the world.

To the *Daily News*, however, the "main issue" of the 1940 campaign was Roosevelt's violation of the "two term principle," which opened "the gates of America wide to the flood of despotism that is inundating most of the rest of the world.'' With a good conscience, therefore, citizens whose taxes were at a twenty-year low could resoundingly reject a president whose policies had visibly improved their city and replenished their pockets.

The majority (54 percent) of those pockets, according to the 1940 census, still belonged to women, who outnumbered men in every adult age bracket. Moreover, 40 percent of them were listed in the labor force,

a percentage reached by no other community in the state. Overall, the population had increased since 1930 by 10 percent, to over 29,000, with the steadily declining ratio of foreign born now under 10 percent for the first time since 1850. And less than a third of these were Germans. Blacks, on the other hand, had increased to over 1,200, or 4 percent of the city's population. With construction on the increase in both city and university, and several industries once again working at capacity—Hoover, for example, was operating three shifts six days a week in the summer of 1940 in order to fill English war orders—Ann Arbor looked once more like a good place for blacks to find work. And it was. Of blacks in the labor force in 1940, 79 percent were employed at regular jobs and another 9 percent on WPA or other public emergency works. This left 12 percent seeking work, half the number searching in most other cities. Ann Arbor also had a perceivable Jewish community, estimated at about 250, not including university faculty and students. For decades after 1880 there had been only a smattering of Jews, not even enough to organize religious services. Even after a rabbi arrived in Ann Arbor in 1915 there had been no settled place of worship; services were held where space was available: the Salvation Army quarters, the Ladies Library, and Schwaben Hall.

But the largest (though still federally uncounted) group of the population were the students, ever young, ever spirited, and ever absorbed in the self-concerned responsibilities of college life.

If their lives were less idyllic than they seemed, their cares were largely bounded by the small world in which they lived. In the autumn of 1940, however, some of the 12,000 enrolled were focusing on distant, larger realities. Europe and Asia were ablaze, and the issue of America's responsibilities was daily debated. The Ann Arbor National Defense Committee, for example, made up of townspeople and faculty, campaigned to overcome the arguments of the isolationists, the pacifists, and the indifferent. Chief among its spokesmen was the aged and redoubtable William Hobbs. Other echoes of 1917-1918 were also evident.

AN OPEN LETTER

Certain vicious and untrue rumors being circulated in Ann Arbor accusing me of disloyalty to the United States of America and my own American Citizenship prompts me to write and publish this open letter in as conspicuous a manner as possible.

I was, like many others in this community, born in Germany. However, I became an American Citizen by naturalization proceedings which were completed on February 4, 1931. My wife became a citizen of this country on November 4, 1931. Having prospered in a small measure, I am and have for several years been a taxpayer in this city. My two boys attend the local public schools.

I am not a member of the German-American Bund nor any Un-American Society or Organization. Despite the malicious statements which are being made by certain persons with the intention of embarrassing me and injuring my restaurant business, I have not been accused by any local, state or United States officer or authority of any Un-American activities or Un-Americanism of any sort. Although I am informed that it is being said upon the streets and elsewhere in the City, that I have been examined by agents of our Federal Government and even that I have been detained in jail, the truth is that I have not, and my place of business and my home have not, even been visited by any such agents, nor have I received any notice from any authority to report to any bureau, court or tribunal whatever to answer to any questions regarding my conduct as an American citizen.

In the spirit of fairness, I ask that any person or persons who have any challenge to make of my conduct and behavior as an American citizen come out in the open and make their complaint to the proper authorities. I am ready and willing that such authorities examine me as to my entire life, past and present, as well as that of the members of my family. In the meantime I appreciate the many assurances of confidence which I have received from my friends in all walks of life in Ann Arbor. All that I ask is that you who may not know me, refrain from repeating idle gossip and that you ascertain the truth of any statements made relative to the matters suggested in this letter. My creed is now, as it has always been since I came to live among you, to be a good husband and father, an honest business man, a law abiding citizen and above all a patriotic AMERICAN.

Sincerely yours,

William "Bill" Metzger,

Metzger's Restaurant.
203 E. Washington St.,
Ann Arbor, Michigan.

Several days later (June 14, 1940) Metzger ran a second letter thanking the many citizens who had expressed their confidence in him, including some who "unthinkingly aided in spreading the slanderous rumor about me." Rumors also had citizens of German ancestry being arrested by the FBI, and a short wave radio communicating directly to Berlin. But Metzger's

126

challenge and the ridicule of local journalists seem to have silenced such gossip. So, perhaps, did the consciences of older, once overeager, patriots.

Neither words nor memories, however, could keep the Germans from invading the Soviet Union in June of 1941, or the Japanese from bombing Pearl Harbor six months later. News of the latter attack, arriving first by radio and then quickly spread by two Sunday afternoon extras of the *Ann Arbor News*, stunned the city as it did the rest of the country. Suddenly there were no more debates about neutrality, only plans for a war come perilously close. Not since the Civil War had the community felt so vulnerable. Armed guards to prevent sabotage immediately appeared in front of the half dozen factories having contracts with the War Department, and plans were drawn up for an auxiliary police, "in the event," explained the police chief, "of attack upon the community." If the Japanese could bomb Hawaii they could bomb anywhere, and might very well aim for Detroit's defense industries. In such a raid Ann Arbor would not escape.

And so a huge local civil defense program came into being, with hundreds registering to assist in whatever way they could. All city residents were urged to attend a series of lectures at Hill Auditorium describing "methods of self defense against air raids and sabotage by enemy agents," and many bought the new federally underwritten bomb insurance that became available in July of 1942. One local insurance firm sold 150 policies in the first two days.

Blackout procedures were first tested the same month, with Mayor Leigh Young and local police officials observing from a plane overhead. "We expect full cooperation but there are always a few people who try to be independent and they'll have to be brought into line." Dozens were, receiving violation warrants in the subsequent weeks. For many of those who cooperated by extinguishing their lights the test was a sobering warning of what might happen—far more sobering, because of the lingering fear it nourished, than the mock battle between university ROTC units held at Ferry Field as part of a July Fourth "Preparedness Pageant."

Eight years had passed since the city had formally commemorated Independence Day. Now a celebration seemed relevant, even obligatory, as old and young together sought to bear witness to deeply stirred sentiments of patriotism. And in the months ahead virtually everyone volunteered in some way for the war effort. They bought bonds, performed civil defense work, planted victory gardens, and set their tables according to ration books and with the help of local bulletins like *Home Front Cues*. The term "home front" had been coined in the First World War, but for Americans it took on real urgency only in the Second. It meant stretching one's duties and doing without certain goods and pleasures so that the productive capacities of the nation might generate the means to win the war.

A mighty example of those means existed only a few miles away, at the Willow Run bomber plant. Already near completion when the war broke out, it was the largest assembly plant yet built, and by the end of 1943 it was turning out giant B-24s at the rate of more than one per hour. But if Willow Run was a model of American "Can-Do" spirit, it also posed a problem for nearby towns. Thousands of men and women came from outstate and beyond to work in the plant, and their demand for housing bankrupted the market. In Ann Arbor public meetings discussed the problem, a mayor's committee investigated it, groups surveyed to find available rooms and apartments, and city government contemplated and abandoned solutions such as a "tent city" and trailer camps.

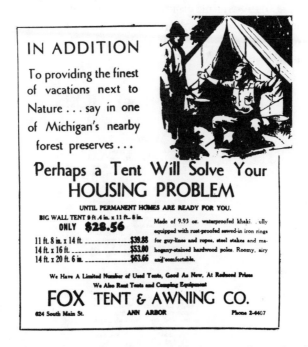

So critical was the problem that some workers were forced to live in their cars while others simply gave up the search (and their jobs) and went back to wherever home had been. Ultimately the State Defense Council told the county that the most important contribution it could make to the war effort would be to find adequate accommodations for the several thousand immigrant workers.

Slowing Ann Arbor's effort to supply housing, argued the *Washtenaw Post Tribune*, was the attitude that the city "is too sweet a place for ordinary men in overalls," especially men who were apt to vote Democratic should they obtain legal residency. But statistics explain more than class or politics. In April 1940 there were 80,000 residents of Washtenaw County; in 1944 there were 106,000; and once the war began there had been virtually no new housing built. Moreover, with the inrush of service personnel undergoing training at the university, the Ann Arbor housing market tightened even further. Qualified women, who by 1943 formed the majority of civilian students, were eventually discouraged from enrolling unless they could be guaranteed a room. With the opening in May 1944 of Pittsfield Village, whose occupants were slated to be only war workers, it was hoped the shortage would ease; but at the end of the year the problem was no less acute. Only when Willow Run started cutting back production in the spring of 1945 did the pressure for living space slacken. And only briefly.

Rationing, shortages, and worries over loved ones far away would seem to have made the war years in Ann Arbor a bleak period. For some it was. But for many, perhaps most, it was also an enlivening time. Jobs were available for the asking,

PERMANENT JOBS

FACTORY

At present there are many openings for GIRLS. If you have good eyesight, capable hands, and if you will be faithful, and conscientious in your work and attendance, come in and talk to us about a job. A cooperative attitude is smetimes more valuable than experience.

There are several openings for MEN: one Mechanical Assembler, One Janitor, and possible replacement jobs in Machine Shop in the near future. One Tool and Die Maker is urgently and permanently needed.

OFFICE

Openings for men: Mechanical Design Engineers, Optical Design Engineers, One Time-Study Engineer and one Chemical Engineer. Openings for women: One Stenographer, One Bookkeeper-Typist and one Optical Computer.

● ANNOUNCEMENT ●

The corporate name of International Industries. Inc., has been changed to:

Argus, Incorporated

and wages were high, so that at Christmas 1942 shoppers "stripped the shelves" of many merchants. Later, price freezes on such things as rents and restaurants stretched earnings even further. And like soldiers at the front, people shed responsibilities that did not seem to matter. Voter apathy, for example, reached a new record: in the city elections of 1944 less than a thousand residents bothered to vote, and a month later a unique town meeting called to determine the tax rate mustered less than five hundred citizens.

The war itself, reported so immediately, so pictorially, and so voluminously, took on the semblance of a real life serial once the first dark months had passed. Confidence in victory steadily grew, while reports of horror were by and large filtered through a government-censored media and a self-censoring national optimism. It was an angry, frustrated Lieutenant Tom Harmon who returned to Ann Arbor in February of 1944 to tell the citizens at a bond rally that "they did not know what war is," and to rebuke them for believing it a "grand adventure" rather than as "the dirtiest, lousiest, muckiest business known." Had Americans the fighting spirit of the Chinese, the former gridiron hero continued, "the war could be over in six months—as it is, we'll be lucky to get out in three years." A city poll taken the month before, in which 74 percent of the men thought Hitler would be defeated by spring or summer, seemed to support Harmon's cry to "wake up." It also may explain why the International White Cross, founded in Ann Arbor in June of 1943 to teach people not to follow leaders who preached nationalistic aggression, drew so little support. But if citizen somnolence or confidence prevailed right up to victory, it did so because of an unyielding patriotism. Memorial Day 1945 found young and old standing in honor, remembrance, and pride.

Three months later the war was over, and in the eyes of many an era in the city's history was as well. Already plans were being drawn up for a new civic center, including new county and city buildings, sponsored by a new mayor, William E. Brown, who also urged extension of the city limits to meet anticipated postwar problems. Growth was on everyone's mind, for it was obvious that the university, as it had after earlier wars, would be expanding, and local factories were expecting to as well. Also being weighed were a variety of recent challenges to the status quo: juvenile delinquency—among "old established families," not late-arriving immigrants—had become a serious problem in the course of the war, forcing the council to write an ordinance and set a curfew; a black man, John Ragland, had run (and lost) in a contest for alderman in the spring of 1945; parking meters, bitterly fought over but not installed in 1938, were finally to be set up in the business districts; and a local attorney, William A. Lucking, was suing the university for failure to pay for fire and police protection. As if to symbolize the passing of more traditional ways, a barn fire killed all the horses of the Ann Arbor Dairy Company two weeks after V-J Day. The next morning, and thereafter, deliveries were made with trucks obtained from Detroit. So prompt an adjustment befitted a business wishing to survive. But a community is generally much slower to respond to challenges and much less able to ignore its past; inertia is its mode of being, especially when it enjoys a strong sense of identity. In the years after 1945 Ann Arbor would grow and change dramatically, more than many citizens desired, yet less than many imagined. For the moment, though, it was still a green, enduring landscape, especially when viewed through a lens, from afar.

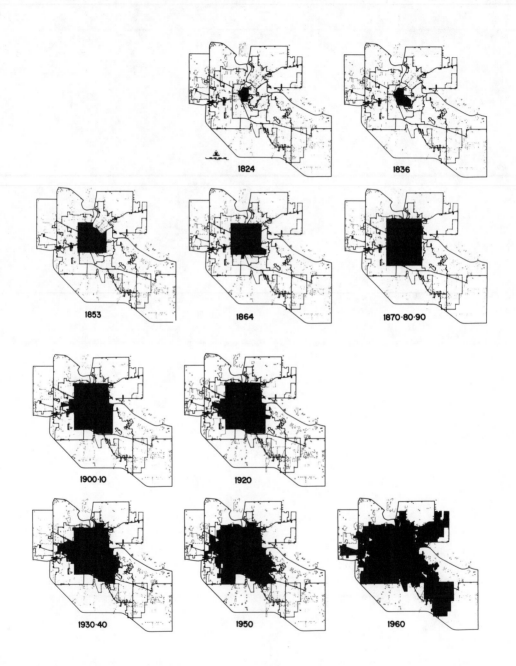

1824

1836

1853

1864

1870·80·90

1900·10

1920

1930·40

1950

1960

Chapter 5

Research Center of the Midwest

1945-1980

Coming home in 1945 to shady streets and Victorian homes, a returning veteran saw much the same town his father had in 1918, or even his grandfather in 1898. Apart from the university, Ann Arbor displayed a turn-of-the-century comeliness, its charms slightly faded but still capable of enchanting residents and transients alike, and of inspiring profound feelings of security. Even the dimensions of the city had changed little in fifty years. The growth in area that marked Ann Arbor's first thirty years, when it promised to become a vigorous commercial and industrial center, had ceased after the Civil War when the university became the pivot for the town's economy and identity. Yet while barely a thousand acres were added to the city's size between 1870 and 1940, tens of thousands of people had entered its population. In 1870 the *real* population (permanent residents plus students) was 7,400; in 1940 it was 40,000. One consequence of these numbers was a dwindling supply of housing lots within the city limits; another was a tax base that without punishing assessments would be unable to keep up with rising city costs. Together these consequences explain why in the fifteen years following World War II Ann Arbor doubled in area.

But in 1945 the future for returning veterans was now, and some could not find a place to live. The wartime shortage in housing did not end in 1945; it grew worse, aggravated by huge postwar student enrollments that

135

saw the numbers jump from 12,000 in the autumn of 1945 to 19,000 a year later and peak at over 21,000 in 1948. Requests for help in finding housing poured into City Hall, including one from former mayor and now Lieutenant Colonel Walter C. Sadler. "Whatever . . . is available we will be pleased to take." To his predecessor's plea as well as to the others, Mayor William E. Brown offered little hope. The housing shortage was not to be quickly made up, especially at a time when building materials were in short supply, and in a city where lots for low- and middle-income housing were at a premium. Making matters worse was that owners of larger homes were unwilling to lease unused space. "Practically all of the rooms that have been made available," reported a survey done in early 1946, "are found in the humbler homes in Ann Arbor."

The crisis was to subside only gradually in the next several years, as home and apartment building began to reach prewar levels and the university made additions to existing dormitories and built others, notably South Quadrangle. A city structure of like capacity (1,200) was apparently in Mayor Brown's mind in 1947 when he tried to persuade the Metropolitan Life Insurance Company of New York to "start a project in Ann Arbor similar to the project on the East River except on a much smaller scale." Both the mayor's idea and the university's reality foreshadowed buildings yet to rise.

While city and university struggled with insufficient housing, they struck a landmark bargain in their relations with each other. In the past the university had paid water and sewer rates, but city officials saw its expanding, tax-exempt presence—the original 40 acres had grown to 360, or 8 percent of city land—an increasingly serious, and unfair, restriction on revenues. A more equitable arrangement was called for, with the city threatening to double the university's water and sewage rates if equity was not achieved. Thus, in September of 1946, after months of difficult negotiations in the shadow of the Lucking suit, an agreement was worked out whereby the university agreed to pay almost $100,000 to assist in the expansion of the city's water or sewage disposal plant facilities, $7,500 in exchange for discontinuing a long-standing free-bed arrangement for city employees, and an annual sum equal to the pay of seven policemen. At last it looked as if the city would be adequately reimbursed for the services it rendered the university. Some council members, though, were angry with Mayor Brown's less than "perfect deal": the sums the city was to receive seemed low, and in the case of the free-bed payment, "ridiculously low." Nonetheless an important precedent had been set: the university, while still not legally bound to contribute to the city, had moved a step beyond being merely another rate payer. It had entered into a complex contractual arrangement that recognized responsibility for paying a share of local government. And in the years ahead the terms of the agreement would be extended to include payments for fire protection. No longer was the university to be treated like a rich relation from whom it was deemed unseemly to ask for room and board.

Rich and poor alike in the city, however, were now being taxed to park their cars. After years of debate and postponements the first parking meters went into operation in June of 1946, adding one more expense (and clock) to city life. Within a few years they were raising upwards of $6,000 per month and allegedly "making the traffic move and thereby helping the merchant." Success with meters begat a unique and far more ambitious experiment: self-supporting city parking structures, paid for by meter and parking revenues. The ordinance permitting the issuance of the revenue bonds to build the structures was passed in August 1947, and in May 1949 a celebration worthy of a great victory took place when the first one was officially opened.

Soon Mayor Brown, the promulgator of the idea, was being showered with requests for information from municipalities across the country hoping to solve their own parking problems. Ann Arbor had attained an unusual first, to hindsight perhaps a prosaic one. But like the agreement with the university, it was an accomplishment that demonstrated the mayor's determination "to run this city like a business."

Such had been Brown's campaign theme in 1945 when, as the wealthy owner of an insurance company, auto agency, and several downtown buildings, he had decided at the age of forty-nine to run for public office. With his grandiose vision of a civic center to include a new county building and city hall, he quickly struck observers as dynamic and imaginative, a mayor who would transform a traditionally "thankless and passive office." And for the twelve years he served, twice as long as any of his usually faceless predecessors, the last three of whom had been university faculty or staff, he was certainly a man of plans and projects. Many of them, like the parking system and the eventually abandoned civic center, were intended to revive a downtown that, to Brown's mind, had "deteriorated tremendously in the last twenty years."

Brown also sought to attract industry "of the right type" so as to strike a more even balance in the town's economy, negotiated tirelessly in difficult situations where city concerns and services were at stake, as with the Veterans Administration over the new hospital, and was the driving force behind annexation efforts. These culminated in 1956 when Ann Arbor swallowed not only three hundred acres of the university's North Campus area but an entire city, East Ann Arbor, with its 655 acres and two thousand residents. Never before had Ann Arbor been served by a mayor who gave so much of his time and spent so much of his money ($75,000, by his own account, in twelve years) in the service of the city, and the grateful citizens returned him to office with ever-increasing majorities, climaxing in 1953 when he swept every precinct. Voters also regularly returned Republican majorities to the council as Democratic strength in the city sank below 40 percent.

No small part of Brown's popularity stemmed from his accomplishing, or taking credit for accomplishing, things that cost no tax dollars. Projects that did fared less well. Citizens who had watched their city taxes drop in the 1930s and rise only gradually during the war were willing in the postwar era to be taxed for such self-evident needs as more schools. But their rejection in 1950 of an increase in the mill limit on property taxes demonstrated that they were loathe to let the city spend freely. And as federal taxes and inflation rose, they began saying no to what the mayor proposed, frequently in the case of a new City Hall and dramatically in February 1957 when they rejected each of six proposals in a $3.8 million capital improvement program intended to provide necessary services for the rapidly expanding city. Two months later Mayor Brown, stamped by his Democratic opponent as a "champion of high taxes," lost his bid for re-election. At the time, Ann Arbor's total property taxes (city, school, and county) were surpassed by five other lower peninsula cities among sixteen selected at random for comparison.

Dynamic as Brown was, Ann Arbor's growth in the postwar years was not driven by his policies and personality, or even by the ambitions of the business and real estate interests that supported him. The real engine powering growth was the university. It was the university that opened its doors to thousands of students, that in 1950 acquired the land for a second campus north of the city limits, and that charted a future in which reseach would increasingly define its purpose. Each of these acts by itself significantly influenced the city's development; together, and over time, they had an enormous impact, far more than the enrollment-generated growth spurts that followed earlier wars. Additional students and additional buildings had in the past stoked the town's economy and enhanced its architecture, but the university's metamorphosis from essentially a teaching into a research-oriented institution—a change observable simply in the names given postwar buildings—would reshape Ann Arbor's economy. Industry of "the right type," long desired and occasionally found (Argus Camera), now became a burgeoning reality—not because the city itself was suddenly discovered to be attractive,

"I did it with my little magnet!"

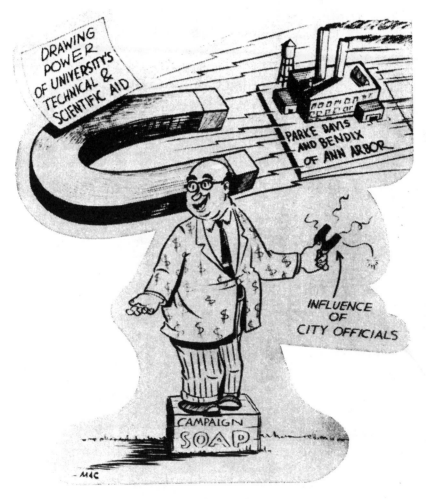

but because the university's new mission, increasingly subsidized by federal contracts and grants, conformed to the interests and needs of research-intensive corporations. And in some instances the research itself inspired faculty members to become entrepreneurs and start up their own companies. The city cooperated by annexing lands, zoning for use, and supplying services; the development of the Greater Ann Arbor Research Park on its southern edge symbolized its commitment. But its actual role—as with the Veterans Hospital, lured really by the proximity of the medical center—was usually that of an accommodating, grateful beneficiary.

Predictably, the city's growth after World War II prompted another attempt to revise the charter. The very age of the much-amended document seemed to demand its replacement, and so did the city's substantial growth.

A NEW CITY CHARTER IS UP TO YOU

IN 1889 ANN ARBOR HAD 8000 POPULATION AND AN ANNUAL BUDGET OF $40,000— IN 1949 ANN ARBOR HAS 40,000 POPULATION — AND AN ANNUAL BUDGET OF $1,000,000

Yet earlier efforts at revision—the latest in 1939, when citizens vetoed even the creation of a charter commission—did not augur success. Nor did the mayor's reluctance to see what he termed a "sacred document" much more than brushed and smoothed. But the desire to restructure city government for greater efficiency and accountability had determined, if not exactly mass, support—only 10 percent of those eligible went to the polls in 1953 to elect commission members. And when the commission went to work two weeks later, its open and temperate hearings, to which citizens were invited to offer their views, earned support for its purpose. So did its deliberate, even cautious, progress as it moved from a consideration of further "piecemeal" amendments to a unanimous vote (March 1954) to revise the charter completely, though without creating a "revolutionary" document.

What emerged from the commission, however, imagined a thorough if not radical reorganization of city government. The seven wards were reduced to five, with the council thereby reduced to ten members; the office of council president was abolished and the mayor officially returned to the body of the council and given a vote; a new office, city administrator, was established to oversee the work of the various city departments; and, finally, several of the citizen boards mandated under the old charter to advise city departments were discontinued. This last change so irritated Mayor Brown that shortly before the new charter was to come up for citizen approval (April 1955), he broke with his own party's support of the charter and departed from his stand of "neither endorsing nor working against it." At a public meeting he denounced the elimination of the boards: cutting people out of government was a step closer to "that communist business." While known for his plain-spokenness and bluff patriotism—in December 1947 he had revoked the permission previously given by the Parks Department for a communist to speak in Felch Park— Brown's comment still outraged a number of people. So did his reply to a fellow Republican's charge that he was "among the first to bring gutter politics" to Ann Arbor: "[I] have to look into this fellow's background." But this last-minute threatmongering could not stall the momentum of a document supported by both political parties and the local newspapers. With the city expanding every which way, a remodeled government seemed obligatory, and in record numbers the voters gave their approval. In April of 1956 it officially went into effect.

In the process of taking testimony for the charter, the commission had been addressed by Albert Wheeler, a black research scientist at the university and a member of the Ann Arbor Civic Forum. This was an inter-racial group devoted to examining and eliminating racial bias by "every moral and legal effort." Rarely before could any of the members of the all-white commission (comprised of four university faculty, three businessmen, an attorney, and a housewife) have heard their city so unsparingly criticized for its "willful . . . discriminatory patterns" in public and private employment, in housing, and in health care. "To deny the existence of widespread active discrimination in Ann Arbor is to admit naivete, ignorance, bigotry, or indifference." It scarcely mattered that a black had finally been elected to the council in 1953—the same year the first woman won a seat—or that a full-time black teacher had recently been hired into the school system. In the eyes of the Civic Forum and the NAACP, a local chapter of which had been newly organized in 1949, the exceptional cases only underlined the rule; tokenism only evaded the problem. Along with a new charter Ann Arbor needed a Human Relations Commission to investigate complaints and institute community educational programs.

Three years later it had one, created with the bipartisan support of the council under Mayor Brown's successor, Samuel J. Eldersveld. What it found was what it had been told it would find: blatant discrimination in employment and especially in housing, where the pattern of segregation made it almost impossible for a black and very difficult for an oriental to buy or rent in white neighborhoods. (Since the war foreign students, most of whom were graduate students and thus not eligible for dormitory space, had found themselves regularly turned away by city landlords.) However well blacks had done in Ann Arbor, and however much respect they were accorded by some townspeople, their lives had been bound within understood limits: they worked in largely unskilled, blue-collar jobs, lived almost exclusively in a half-dozen areas on the north side and along the river, and knew they would be ignored or insulted if they entered certain restaurants. Mayors and university presidents might speak in their churches, and the newspapers record their activities, but in the minds of many residents they had neither standing nor respect.

To be sure, Ann Arbor had been a tolerable and occasionally, for some blacks, more than a tolerable community. But in the throes of a great national awakening to civil rights, as television images of federal troops in Little Rock broke into consciences, what had been tolerable was being redefined as intolerable. The determination to change habits and assumptions was disquieting, and in a city of proud homeowners, rising property values, and prosperous realtors, the prospect of a rules change in housing was deeply threatening.

Even while the Human Relations Commission was undertaking its investigation—and quietly working outside "normal channels" to assist minority group home-seekers—virtually the entire citizenry of Ann Arbor was debating a momentous decision: Should the north central area, comprising 74 acres, 342 structures, and 502 families (some 1,700 individuals) undergo urban renewal?

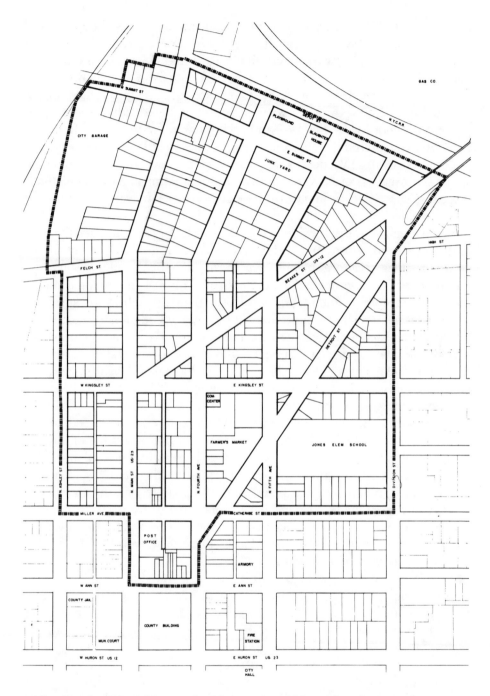

Talk of revitalizing the area had begun in 1955, and a plan was drawn up and application for funding submitted to the federal government. A grant of almost $1 million was approved, with the city being left responsible for another $250,000. Under this original plan, major reconstruction would have taken place, but the prospect of bulldozer leveling roused a frenzy of opposition, and a new plan emphasizing building rehabilitation was designed. This too, however, met hostile fire, both from many who lived in the area—like the Reverend C.W. Carpenter of Second Baptist Church who thought it was "morally wrong" and "exploited" the residents, 70 percent of whom were blacks—and those, like the Ann Arbor Board of Realtors, who feared its economic consequences. And then there were opponents like George Wedemeyer, who owned property in the area but who spoke against the project, as he told a Kiwanis meeting in November 1958, "because it is socialistic in nature. It places too much power in the hands of a few people."

Spokesmen on the other side, led by Mayor Eldersveld, likened the plan to democracy in action, and had the support of some of the area residents as well as such civic organizations as the League of Women Voters, the Chamber of Commerce, and the Council of Churches, not to mention the 2,500 citizens who signed a petition in the plan's behalf in the spring of 1959. Indeed, not since temperance in its heyday had an issue so bitterly divided the citizens, and temperance had not probed the kinds of financial, ideological, and racial feelings engendered by urban renewal. Indicative of how deep and widespread was the concern is that a public hearing and city council meeting held on the issue in December 1958 were broadcast live over local radio—a first in the city's history. Six months later, with time running out on the availability of federal funds, the council voted 6 to 5 in favor of the project. But the victory was only temporary. One of the five losing votes belonged to the new mayor, Cecil Creal, and several days later he exercised his veto power on the grounds that the plan would be too disruptive. Efforts to override failed, and instead of federal urban renewal Ann Arbor got a Neighborhood Rehabilitation and Improvement Committee, which in its first annual report listed five substandard homes razed and five completely remodeled. Thus, piecemeal, was begun a very gradual process of rejuvenation.

Despite growth and division, Ann Arbor in the 1950s still held on to some of the dreams and even some of the realities of being a small, homogeneous town. By 1960 there were 67,000 inhabitants, but more than a third of this number were students—counted since 1950 in the federal census. Downtown there was finally a new County Building, after years of squabbling with Ypsilanti over the location, and a site being readied for a new City Hall, finally approved by the voters. But there was still no new hotel, and Main Street, little changed for decades, had as yet no shopping centers to compete with. Around the university and in the various subdivisions construction was booming; over a thousand new

homes had been built in 1955 alone, and almost yearly a new elementary school opened to meet the mounting demand for classroom space.

But construction had often boomed without changing the essential rhythms of the community. Certainly Ann Arbor was physically becoming something other than what it had been, a metamorphosis enacted in the emergence of the new County Building,

whose simple, utilitarian architecture did not even pretend to inspire civic pride. But the transformation in habits and attitudes was to be much slower. The town's voting behavior was still thoroughly Republican, with Adlai E. Stevenson losing twice to Dwight D. Eisenhower by more than two to one, John F. Kennedy doing scarcely better against Richard Nixon, and Democrats (like Eldersveld) in local or state elections having to rely on serendipitous factors if they hoped to carry the city. Only twice in forty years (1926, 1940) had Ann Arbor gone Democratic in gubernatorial elections, while before 1957 the last Democrat to sit in the mayor's chair had been Edward Staebler (1927-1931). Moreover, the comments of Mayor Brown or George Wedemeyer about "communistic" and "socialistic" undertakings could be reproduced endlessly, for in the 1950s Ann Arbor was still a very religious and patriotic town where on Sundays shops closed and churches filled—including First Methodist on State Street where for almost half the decade a university student from Singapore, embarrassed by his low grades, hid among the rafters. Also on a Sunday you were apt to see Mayor Creal driving around town and talking to people to determine what needed to be done. Or you might go to a local park, cherished symbol of civic improvement, and enjoy an afternoon away from the world.

Sitting there preoccupied with their delight, this couple would not have let worldly events interrupt their amorous moment, any more than they would have imagined that in the next decade disease would strip Ann Arbor of many of its beloved trees, or that dissent would rip apart its fabled calm and transform its image from a quiet and significant university town into a noisy and inspiring center of political activism, a place where presidents and protestors set out national agendas.

The tone was set late one October night in 1960 when presidential candidate John F. Kennedy, speaking from the steps of the Michigan Union, asked the largely student crowd if they would contribute a year or two of their lives to public service. Quoting Bismarck, he offered a new kind of role to the young in shaping the country's future; his words also implicitly encouraged the students to examine what the country was at present. Less than four years later Lyndon Johnson called upon a commencement gathering of 85,000 in the Michigan Stadium to fight "to end poverty and racial injustice" in order to achieve "the great society." His words were enthusiastically cheered, for like Kennedy he offered a splendid vision to the right audience at a time when it was assumed that the best and brightest could accomplish what they would.

Neither man, however, took much notice of *where* he actually was. Kennedy neglected to mention Ann Arbor ("I am delighted to come to Michigan, to the university"), while Johnson scarcely set foot in it,

arriving and departing by helicopter immediately outside the stadium. Perhaps both men had been told that the city was incorrigibly Republican and not worth stroking. (Franklin Roosevelt had only "smiled a cheery, 'good morning' " to a crowd of three hundred people while his train sat on a siding for four hours in 1932.) But their oversight more likely derived from the common outsider's perception that the university *was* the city, that the streets, the buildings, and the people of Ann Arbor were, in effect, one large support system for the university. Once wide of the truth, that perception now seemed in the eyes of some residents to be uncomfortably close. As large as the town had grown, the university had seemed to grow even larger, even more influential, and even more intrusive into the lives of the residents. In the words of an Oxford Road homeowner, complaining of the dormitory complex going up there in 1962, the university was "going its way with increasing contempt for the city, the laws, and the individuals who live in the city."

Earlier citizen complaints about the university had usually focused either on instances of student misbehavior, which were soon forgotten, or on issues like the 1928 dormitory project, which could be resolved by compromise and/or soothing rhetoric. But now citizens were complaining about the university as such, as a colossus out of control managed by bureaucrats indifferent to the consequences of its expansion. "Do you think we could have accomplished what we have if we had to meet with the city everytime we wanted to do something?" Expressions like that confirmed fears that the city's "biggest industry" might become its "biggest threat." Forgotten in such worries was that the university's presence had for decades kept Ann Arbor green and quiet and leisurely, and that its postwar growth and orientation were a response to challenges impossible to ignore. If the university had outgrown both the city and the outlook of its residents (not to mention its own alumni), it did so because it wanted to continue as a premier institution, worthy of Tappan's dream and of Kennedy's witty reference to his own alma mater, Harvard, as "the Michigan of the East."

Ann Arbor's growth in the 1950s had meant extended boundaries and increased population; its growth in the 1960s brought a different face and spirit. It would go from being a small city with a small-town feeling to being still a small city but with large-city aspirations. (In 1953 the League of Women Voters published a sixty-page pamphlet entitled *Know Your Town*; in 1977 the pamphlet was expanded to ninety-five pages and re-titled *Know Your City*.) Shopping centers were laid out on the periphery, and while they siphoned off customers from downtown stores, they poured welcome dollars into city coffers. Buildings rose in the center of the city

148

that mocked its lone 1929 "skyscraper" and dwarfed earlier towers (fire, church, and bell) built to human scale. Sophisticated shops and restaurants, catering to diverse and moneyed tastes, appeared and disappeared. And a politics of principle and confrontation, energized by national and global issues, tried to use and identify the city as a place of justice.

Few residents cheered all of these developments; even fewer deplored all of them. Many did not even recognize the loss of the familiar, for they had arrived in the midst of the changes. Between 1950 and 1970 Ann Arbor's population more than doubled, from 48,000 to 100,000, a result primarily of in-migration (including students) rather than annexation or a higher than average birthrate. These newcomers had no attachments to the city as it had been and thus usually offered little resistance to its being altered. To them, as to settlers a century before, Ann Arbor was an attractive location that asked to be and, for some, needed to be improved—not merely enjoyed for what it was. A majority of these people were young and many were drawn by the university—enrollments rose from 24,000 to 32,000 between 1960 and 1970, while the instructional staff grew from 2,500 to 4,300. Others came to work in the local research and development firms. By 1965 research was the city's fastest growing "industrial" activity in terms of employment. Boosters took notice and began describing Ann Arbor as "The Research Center of the Midwest."

These newcomers also explain a significant statistical change: in 1950 slightly more than one-third of the male residents over the age of twenty-five were college graduates, and about one-third of the female residents had attended college; by 1960 the figure in each category had risen to almost one-half. No simple conclusions can be deduced from those figures, except that a populace so well educated was expected to react thoughtfully and responsibly by those who asked something of it.

Perhaps an even more noticeable fact about the city's population was that it was undergoing a leavening not seen since the arrival of the Germans. In 1950 there were 1,085 blacks living in Ann Arbor, only 145 more than in 1930. Ten years later (1960) their number had climbed to almost 3,200, close to 5 percent of the total population, but 7 percent of the city's permanent residents, since only a tiny proportion of the university was black—eleven of the 2,105 seniors pictured in the 1962 *Michiganensian*. And in the next decade their number would double. A similar pattern is found among Jews, who numbered about 250 in 1940, not counting university students and faculty, but many times that by 1970, as opportunities for professional careers in law, medicine, and at the university opened up. And it was primarily the university that was luring Asian immigrants (or their children) to Ann Arbor, so that by 1970 they numbered over a thousand. What had once been a white, largely Protestant, and conservative community was still that, but less obviously and less confidently. Other voices were being heard, voices speaking of equality and opportunity, as well as of parks and schools and of how and where liquor should be sold. (Liquor by the glass was voted to businesses west of Division in 1960, while the "dry island" to the east was abolished in 1969.) And these new voices spoke of costs not only in dollars but in dignity and fairness. Their influence was not sufficient in 1963 to pass a "strong" Fair Housing ordinance, but their passion set the framework for the compromise ordinance—the first of its kind in the state.

The approach of the Human Relations Commission to bias in the housing market had been to educate and conciliate, and to hope that those in the city who were quietly working outside ''normal channels'' to assist minority group home-seekers would be successful. Others, especially the Ann Arbor Fair Housing Association, which picketed for eight months in 1961 to obtain an open occupancy agreement with the management of Pittsfield Village Apartments, had developed a more activist strategy. In March of 1962 the city council unanimously passed a resolution declaring that discrimination based on ''race, creed, color, or national origin is a violation of the public policy of the city.'' Soon the local chapter of the NAACP and other groups were campaigning for a city ordinance on housing, and in June the Human Relations Commission formally recommended to the council that such an ordinance be adopted. A committee to prepare an ordinance was appointed, and after months of meetings and hearings and sit-ins and marches, an ordinance was passed by a vote of seven to four. Both Democratic council members opposed the measure, agreeing to the widely held view that the ordinance was ''grossly inadequate'' since it applied only to housing of five or more units, or roughly one third of the city total. Yet if not a total victory over housing discrimination, the ordinance did give direction and teeth to a ''public policy,'' and two years later it was amended to include *all* private housing except rooming houses with fewer than four roomers. Moreover, in the same year (1965) a Housing Commission was established (and survived a close and bitter referendum) to meet the city's housing needs, particularly those of low-income residents. In half a decade a new meaning had been given to the title, ''a city of homes.''

151

A new honor as well, for the housing ordinance and Housing Commission were instrumental to Ann Arbor's being named an "All-America City" in March of 1967. The city's official entry application had listed civil rights first among its achievements, before the beautification of the downtown area and provisions for additional parks and recreational grounds. And the awards committee, representing the National Municipal League and *Look* magazine, had been impressed. They were not seeking "model" or "perfect" communities, but those—and there were ten that year in addition to Ann Arbor—that through citizen action rather than government had made "outstanding progress" in one or more areas of "civic betterment." Ann Arbor had shown splendidly. Behind its progress in civil rights were two to three thousand "people," notably the NAACP; behind its downtown improvement were eight hundred "community leaders," led by the Chamber of Commerce; and behind the $2.5 million bond issue for expanded leisure areas—and a simultaneously approved $5.3 million issue for roads—were the voters, who broke decisively from their "hitherto . . . negative record in regard to voted bond issues."

Such citizen involvement promised future improvements; it promised as well, however, new and different disputes about agendas. For a hundred years townspeople had debated development in terms of economic base: should Ann Arbor encourage more industry or accept the primacy of the university? Linked inextricably to this question was the concern for public image, the concern that the university required a special environment in order to flourish. These issues would continue to be argued, but now parties previously uninvolved or not even present intended to widen the debate.

Blacks were one party, students another. For decades young people had come to Ann Arbor to study and play. They lived in the town, shopped and clerked in its stores, relaxed in its parks and saloons, and occasionally rioted in its streets. But much as they were part of the town they seldom concerned themselves with its development. Few could vote in elections, many never ventured west of Main Street, most were preoccupied with their studies and adventures, and despite rising summer enrollments a sizable majority were absent a quarter of the year. This was to change dramatically in the 1960s, when in addition to marching in Alabama and gathering in Washington students sought to realize their dreams of a just republic in the place where they lived on their own. And so Ann Arbor, along with the university, became for them an arena of action. They participated in fair housing demonstrations, obstructed the local draft board and ROTC units, seized a principal thoroughfare in the summer of 1969, and organized themselves into pressure groups—Tenants Union, Black Action Movement, Graduate Employees Organization—to protest conditions in the city and university. Real power to shape the city's future only came, though, when the voting age was lowered and registration requirements eased.

Vietnam released and legitimized much of this activity. Beginning with an organized discussion (''teach-in'') at the university in March of 1965, which by setting the example for a hundred other campuses identified Ann Arbor as a center of protest, the war established itself as a real presence in the city. Controversy raged over its necessity and morality, and as people made their decision(s) about the war, many learned that politics could be more than votes and patronage, and that families and friendships could be torn apart by belief. Demonstrations, marches, neighborhood canvassing, all were used by the war's opponents to argue their case. Twice petition drives tried to place the war on the ballot, to have citizens testify in their community and as a community. In 1967 a Republican-dominated council declared Vietnam an inappropriate subject for a local election; in 1970 a Democratic-dominated council favored a referendum, but a suit ultimately forced the war off the ballot. Nevertheless, a vote of sorts was taken.

VOTE ON VIETNAM

The Ann Arbor City Council—responding to petitions signed by some 3,000 citizens — authorized a referendum on Vietnam for the April 6 election. But an injunction was obtained from a visiting judge, preventing the propositions from appearing on the ballot. -

We believe Ann Arbor citizens should have an opportunity to indicate their feelings about the war in Southeast Asia. Therefore, we are offering an alternative means of expression.

Below is a mail ballot which carries the propositions as they would have appeared on the April 6 ballot.

Vote for one of the four propositions.

Send the mail ballot to:

Vote on Vietnam
Ann Arbor News
Ann Arbor, Michigan 48108

THE ANN ARBOR NEWS will count the votes received by Wednesday, April 15.

153

Those who supported the government, or at least trusted its intentions, also spoke out. When speeches at the university turned into sit-ins at the draft board, a Republican councilman, in anticipation of Veterans Day, offered a resolution supporting U.S. policy and condemning those who used civil disobedience as a means of protest. The proposal was withdrawn before it came to a formal vote, but its appearance recalled the patriotism enlisted during former wars, which would continue to be heard. When, for example, a Moratorium Day was held in 1969 and 20,000 people gathered to hear calls for an end to the ''agony of Vietnam,''

one Main Street merchant hung a banner from his store reading ''Win the War'' while other like-minded townspeople drove their cars with headlights ablaze and flew the flag from their homes.

The divisions in Ann Arbor paralleled those in most communities as Americans coped with a war that touched them so little and yet so much. But once they turned off their television sets and laid aside their newspapers most Americans could escape Vietnam. Not so the residents of Ann Arbor. Consciousness of the war became almost a condition of their lives because questioning the war became so fundamental and public an activity of so many around them. The city in those years became a kind of open classroom, a noisy forum of competing voices and occasional disorder, but

154

a place, too, where education went forward. The teach-in that was to have lasted twelve hours carried on for eight years.

In the midst of the turmoil the city experienced a riotous episode unparalleled in its history. On several successive June nights in 1969 up to a thousand youths, many of them university students, congregated to "liberate" South University Street of automobiles and to turn it into a mall. The incident began on a Monday night as a spontaneous party that broke up on its own, but then reignited on Tuesday and Wednesday nights with the street being blocked and epithets and stones being hurled at city police and local sheriff's deputies, who responded with tear gas and night sticks. In quelling the disturbances, state police as well as sheriff's men from other counties were called in, and they were joined by Mayor Robert J. Harris, university president Robben Fleming, and dozens of faculty members who tried to calm the youths. There were numerous arrests and minor injuries, but unlike the 1890 student skirmish with the local National Guard unit, no one was killed. And property damage, limited to a few broken windows, was less than the Star Theater riot of 1908.

But if not destructive materially, the South University disturbances were deeply unsettling. The challenge to civility and authority was deliberate, and authority, especially in the person of the Washtenaw County sheriff, Douglas Harvey, took up the challenge as if the fate of the city were at stake. It wasn't, and there was withering criticism of the sheriff's "mismanagement." Still, the police reaction was not without logic. For

155

the disturbances, because they grew on themselves and developed demands on the city, posed a different kind of threat than earlier student riots, which, even when they stemmed from an observed, legitimate grievance, had no life beyond the riotous act itself. In 1969 youth and police clashed with a will, each sensing that they were making a necessary political statement, and believing themselves the defenders of virtue.

And when the mayor himself walked the streets trying to ease tempers—his predecessor in 1908 had left matters to those acting *in loco parentis*—and area businessmen threatened to ''move out of Ann Arbor'' if order was not restored, they too sensed the disturbances' larger meanings. In the aftermath there was much debate over the handling of the affair, with many residents complaining of police brutality and many others decrying City Hall meddling with law enforcement. A drive to recall the mayor—the first in city history—was also initiated but eventually foundered of its own ineptitude. The attempt, however, like the disturbances themselves, revealed how custom and authority were being redefined.

In the census of 1970, after correction, Ann Arbor reached a population of just over 100,000. In twenty years it had grown, in the words of the city planning department, "from a small college town . . . to a bustling city," one that now included 50 percent more people and acreage than it had a decade before. Nevertheless, almost 90 percent of its population lived within the 1960 boundaries, evidence of how in-migration and surging student enrollments determined growth, and evidence, too, for why owner-occupied housing had decreased from 52.3 percent in 1950 to 43.8 percent in 1970. Rental housing fit the needs of a population which promised to turn over by 40 percent every five years. A glance at the city's tallest buildings, not to mention its sprawling apartment complexes, reinforced the impression that a city of homes was gradually becoming a city of apartments and condominiums. And more were being planned as developers, despite rising costs and tight money, dreamed of a 12 percent or higher return on their money. By 1976 more than half of the 40,000 dwelling units in the city had been built since the late 1950s. Dreamed of as well was the huge shopping center being planned at the south end of the city on land annexed in June of 1969. Set adjacent to the interstate highway, Briarwood seemed destined to become a regional emporium, drawing customers from well beyond county lines and breaking the century-old habit of local residents going to Detroit to shop—a habit already curbed by the 1967 Detroit riot. And as the mall took shape, so did plans for neighboring structures. Ann Arbor had become big in size and scale and ambition, bigger than its roads and sewage system, for example, could handle, and bigger, it seemed, than its quality of life could survive. In the minds of many the city could not afford continuous growth.

For some this was largely a financial complaint, expressed not only in the opposition to a shopping center likely to savage downtown businesses, but in a wariness about further annexations of outlying properties. Despite the willingness of developers to share in the costs of extending city services to newly annexed land, and despite the revenues that would be raised once those lands were developed, residents increasingly fretted about the costs to the city (and hence themselves) that followed annexations. Twice in 1970, for example, they rejected annexation proposals recommended by city officials, bucking, at least temporarily, the "engrained tradition" of normally easy passage.

Other skeptics of growth argued positions being voiced nationally.

"Does growth guarantee economic well being?" asked the Citizens Association for Area Planning in 1970, and they and the local chapter of the Sierra Club also questioned the wisdom of further "piecemeal development of [the] city without a general development plan." Then there were citizens who felt that bigness would destroy those special qualities of calm, quiet, and beauty that made the town so attractive. Memory knew that Ann Arbor was not what it had been, that the buildings, shopping centers,

and droves of people and cars had changed rhythms and perspectives. But it still seemed possible to save some of the town's traditional ambience. It also seemed necessary, for without the effort the town appeared destined to lose its identity. The steps taken to preserve ambience can be summarized in two words: planning and preservation. The first was realized in the reports that began issuing out of city offices and local organizations, as well as in specific campaigns like the one to control the size and spread of signs; the second in the establishment of neighborhood organizations like the Old West Side Association (1967), and in the passage of a municipal preservation ordinance (1971). Together, it was hoped, they might manage to keep the essence of Ann Arbor intact. Meanwhile, nostalgia was plentiful, and profitable.

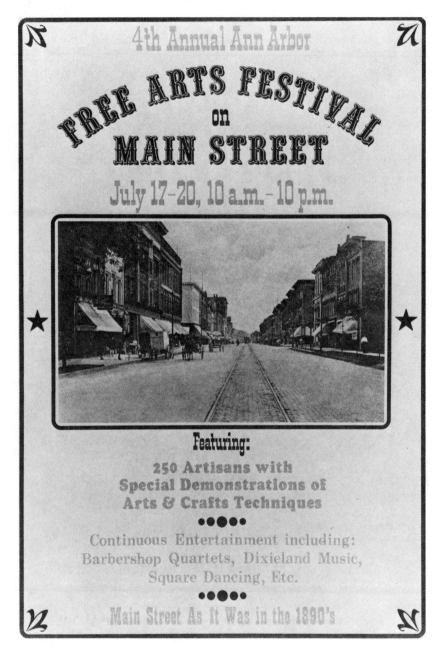

Size, however, was not the only threat to Ann Arbor's ambience. By the early 1970s it seemed to some residents that the students posed an even more insidious threat. With their politics, their music, their drugs, and their liberated sexuality, they were easily stereotyped as a nuisance or worse, and their behavior condemned and lamented. "Now the students are going down the same path that caused the Roman Empire to fall," a police detective had warned in 1967. "If they don't like a law they rebel against it. The students are trying to make themselves a group immune to the law." How could the authorities keep order if the source of disorder was not in reachable, traditional adversaries like the bars but in the *will* of those to be protected?

Even worse seemed to be the young people gathered around John Sinclair, founder of the White Panther political party (subsequently the Rainbow People) and of an underground newspaper that delighted in scandalizing middle-class values.

ANN ARBOR
TRIBAL COUNCIL

July 14   8:00 p.m.
627 Mary St. (Mary St. Project)
SERVE THE PEOPLE

In their politics Sinclair and his followers were not so much radical as antinomian. Their rock concerts were political statements as well as musical offerings—and detested as either by townspeople proud of the city's musical tradition. Nothing in Ann Arbor's past quite paralleled their behavior, yet all of Ann Arbor's past explained its existence. They were the heirs, recognized or not, of numerous earlier crusaders, whose causes had been clearer and whose dress (and language) more conventional, but whose harsh attacks on the status quo had also outraged citizens. With its perennially young and educated population, Ann Arbor naturally attracted and nurtured idealists and dissenters. And though abolitionists had been attacked, and temperance folk and socialists frustrated at the polls, the city had continued to appear as a haven for those with a cause. Only now, with eighteen-year-olds able to vote, it was imaginable to some that Ann Arbor was about to be taken over by a revolutionary ethos. The dreams of John Allen and Henry Tappan seemed to be spinning into a nightmare.

Heretofore students had played only a minor role in city elections. Even those twenty-one and older—a growing segment after World War II as the proportion of graduate students rose to almost 50 percent—often were denied the franchise by deliberately restrictive rules. Now they stood to be the most powerful and most liberal bloc in a city that already was shedding its conservative color. Lyndon Johnson had beaten Barry Goldwater by almost two-to-one in the 1964 presidential election, and Hubert Humphrey had been given a narrow three hundred vote majority in 1968, five months before Robert Harris won the mayor's office for the Democrats for only the second time since 1931. Democrats also won a significant majority on the council (8-3), turning a fifteen-year trend that had seen Republicans win sixty-eight of the eighty-nine council seats up for election. The key to Harris's victory were the 9,000 new registered voters since 1967, voters registered in large part by student volunteers. Both the Harris and Eldersveld victories were termed major upsets, but in fact they registered a seismic political shift.

The real shock, however, one that staggered liberals as well as conservatives, was felt three years later in the spring election of 1972. Voters in the First and Second wards each elected to the council a member of the Human Rights Party (HRP), a radical coalition of interests that placed "people and ecology above business" and pledged to leash in the police, the landlords, and City Hall bureaucrats. Overnight, student power became a reality, and townspeople woke up to the prospect that before long almost half of the council could be students elected by students, that the city's temporary residents might dictate its future. The community, many feared, had now gone topsy-turvy in its politics as well as in its values. The passage a few weeks after the election of an ordinance softening the penalties for marijuana possession seemed fully to justify those fears.

161

The marijuana ordinance drew national attention, and letters soon began arriving from city officials asking for copies and information. Twenty years before, similar requests had come in asking about Ann Arbor's new parking system. In each case a proud mayor was happy to oblige, though there was as much difference between the generally brief, ebullient replies of businessman-mayor William E. Brown and the lawyerly answers of professor-mayor Robert Harris as there was between the ordinances themselves and what they seemed to say about the passage of time. A year later a Republican mayor and Republican council repealed what they viewed as a noxious ordinance. But theirs was not the last judgment. In April of 1974, thanks to a petition drive by the HRP and to the voters of the two predominantly student wards, the $5 marijuana penalty was restored, this time in the city charter and so not reachable by council action. Despite renewed fears of the effect of such license, Sodom did not materialize, though on April Fool's Day for several years thereafter crowds of young people, many from other towns, swarmed around the steps of the university library in a smoky rite of celebration.

In the same election (1974) voters were asked to consider another HRP-initiated charter amendment, one with far more serious ramifications: rent control. The proposal called for a rollback of rents to 1973 levels and the establishment of a nine-member commission to rule on increases. As with earlier measures touching property values, like the fair housing ordinance or the university's decision to build dormitories, rent control touched off a bitter debate filled with fanciful claims and apocalyptic warnings. It was also a uniquely expensive battle. The Citizens for Good Housing, an ad hoc opposition group, spent $45,000 to defeat the measure—an extraordinary sum in Ann Arbor politics, where a few thousand dollars could clear a path to a council seat or the mayor's office. When the votes were counted the measure had won in the First and Second wards, but lost heavily in the other three where anxious homeowners, warned by the city assessor that rent control would eventually cost them more in taxes as rental property lost its market (and thus assessed) value, joined forces with fearful real estate and building interests.

A year later, rent control was again on the ballot and again went down to defeat. Exactly how much homeowner fear of higher taxes contributed to either defeat is impossible to gauge, but it was certainly real, and, in an era of national inflation, extended beyond property assessments. Beginning in 1969 with a vote on a city income tax—which would have entailed a lower property tax—Ann Arbor voters had routinely rejected city requests for more general revenue, saying no both on an ''advisory'' vote on an income tax (1972) and on special one-year millage increases (1972 and 1974). It did not seem to matter that the city was running deficits of $1.2 million a year and was (since 1971) receiving several hundred thousand dollars less per year from the university for police and fire protection. Residents believing themselves to live in one of the nation's most expensive communities were very ready to analyze city deficits as a product of waste and mismanagement. Bond issues for dams (1970) and parks (1971), or special assessments for a city transportation system (1973) chronically underfinanced and underused, won passage because the funds were ticketed for specific improvements with desired returns. But when asked to hand money to city officials to spend as they thought necessary, citizens balked. Moreover, city government was now large and layered, an easy target for anyone at a time when distrust of government was endemic. George Wallace, the fiery spokesman for this distrust, garnered 4,300 Ann Arbor votes in the 1972 presidential primary.

Of course residents had a long tradition of being unwilling to tax themselves unless they reaped a tangible benefit. In this regard they were not so different from other communities—except that they sometimes desired improvements, such as $800,000 worth of bike paths (1973), that other cities would have shunned as a luxury; suffered property taxes they imagined (wrongly) no other community experienced; and had the wit and confidence to argue, organize, and demonstrate to effect their will. And with the HRP able to arouse and capitalize on youthful idealism,

Ann Arbor in the early 1970s seemed even more different, not only from towns of like size, but even from other university towns. Arguments over what city government should be doing articulated the deepest political principles, while consensus as to the city's future development seemed beyond reach.

Climaxing this tumultuous period was the 1975 mayoral election, held

under a new preferential voting system that allowed voters the option of ranking candidates. This effectively gave third-party supporters the deciding voice when neither major party won a majority. The system had been passed by the voters in the spring of 1974, thanks once more to an HRP petition drive and heavy majorities in wards One and Two, and much to the disgust of city Republicans, who no longer enjoyed a sizable advantage. "I am opposed to third parties," cried Mayor James Stephenson, himself a beneficiary in 1973 when the HRP had drained off votes from his Democratic opponent. "Show me a well-run country that has third parties."

Five months later Stephenson had cause to be more contemptuous. Reelected by less than 50 percent of those voting, he watched in angry disbelief as the second choice of the HRP voters lifted black Democrat Albert Wheeler past him. Subsequent Republican challenges to the election failed:

Judge Fleming sorts it out

the HRP had scored its greatest—and last—triumph. Two years later, with students cooled to radical causes, the party disappeared into the Socialist fold, and with it went, in the words of a 1974 Republican candidate for council, the spectre of Ann Arbor "being taken over by hippies and faggots." Still, in their seven years the HRP had done at least as much as earlier booster groups to make citizens think about what the city could become, for better or worse. And had they known a key slogan of the Ann Arbor Civic Association—"Let us be so united in our struggle for the ideal human environment that we may be a City with a Conscience"—they could easily have adopted it as their own.

The election of Albert Wheeler, however tainted it may have looked to some residents, came at a fitting moment in the city's history. In the wake of a year-long celebration of its 150th birthday, the tongue-tripping theme of which had been "Ann Arbor 150—From the Past to the Present for the Future," the city now had a black mayor for the first time, someone for whom past, present, and future were not merely words but stations in a lifelong battle. For twenty-five years Wheeler had publicly fought to end discrimination in the city, unafraid to say the things that were so or to criticize solutions that were not. Other blacks, though, had also been "raising hell" in recent years, notably those trying to improve the lives of residents in the north central area under the Model Cities program, and those in the Black Economic Development League, which had begun as a pressure group to extract contributions ("reparations") from area churches

and developed into a respected agency that financed numerous self-help programs. Citizens who had deplored "hippies and faggots" taking over the city were probably no happier when Albert Wheeler took his oath of office. But for many more residents it was a moment of pride.

Wheeler himself should put the reader in mind of John Allen, founder and first village president. Both men had come to the valley of the Huron to realize their dreams, and up to a point succeeded. But where Allen and his contemporaries strove to see the village grow, Wheeler and his were trying to manage development that seemed already to have blighted the town. "Oh, it was a beautiful town," said Wheeler in 1976 reminiscing of the 1950s, "acres and acres of trees, big trees. . . . There was a certain charm and peacefulness to that type of community—in contrast to today."

This lament for a lost Eden was decades old, and in the following decade would be sounded even more funereally, as federal tax incentives triggered another building boom, as the northeast quadrant of the city joined the Briarwood area in rapid growth, and as yet another super highway connected the city with the Detroit metropolitan area and brought a step closer the day when Ann Arbor would be swallowed up in a southeast Michigan megalopolis. Citizen protests checked specific projects and the recession of the late 1970s slowed construction, but the pressures and opportunities determining growth remained. Claims that the city was losing its identity were frequently made and rebutted. But the disinterested eye could not fail to notice that the city was losing its streets to overuse and neglect, its indigenous businesses to national chains, and much of its downtown space to the warehouse architecture of parking structures. The last were needed to serve the increasingly large proportion of residents who lived far from where they worked, shopped, and played, far, in some cases, even from sidewalks. By the 1980 census less than one-third of the population dwelled within the area where forty years before virtually everyone had lived. And although the university's postwar development had spawned a varied economy beyond its walls that could profit the city, these new industries, together with the firms they attracted, left Ann Arbor potentially more vulnerable to national economic forces.

Though residents periodically mourn the passing of the city's identity, it has nevertheless remained intact. Perhaps more in the imagination than in reality, but that may always have been true. Settlers attracted by western opportunities, immigrants looking for a fresh start, generations of students seeking an education, researchers looking for answers and technologies—for all of these Ann Arbor has been a place and, in many minds, an inspiration: to arrive here was to begin anew, to find what had not yet been given. And the thousands of temporary visitors who yearly came to have their bodies mended in the city's hospitals or their spirits lifted at concerts, fairs, and football games—for them, too, Ann Arbor was a place of hope, a town that however many residents it numbered played host to many more who would have liked to claim residence. Indeed, however much it has changed and however unnerving its growing sprawl and babel, the city has always had the effect of an idea on residents and visitors, who have imagined its trees and streets and buildings, its very rhythms, to embody a community more wonderful than the sum of its actual parts. And a community more wonderful than most others. As it entered the second half of its second century Ann Arbor was not what it had been, but it survived in the form of what generations had wanted it to be.

ILLUSTRATIONS

Unless otherwise noted, all photographs, maps, and other graphic materials were obtained from the Bentley Historical Library at the University of Michigan. In the case of photographs from the *Ann Arbor News*, the majority of which were taken by Eck Stanger, I was kindly allowed to use the original negatives.

Chapter 1
Page

1. (facing) Plan of Ann Arbor, 1824.

4. Ad for Washtenaw Brewery. *Michigan Emigrant*, November 6, 1834, p. 4.

5. Painting of John Allen.

9. Ad for diorama of Moscow Fire. *Michigan Argus*, August 21, 1850, p. 3.

12. Map of Ann Arbor, 1836. J. F. Stratton.

14. Ann Arbor Land Company handbill, 1837.

16. Photograph of university buildings, 1849. "Records, 1889 and 1899, of the Class of 1849."

17. Ad for Irish relief. *Michigan Argus*, March 3, 1847, p. 3.

20. Census page. Federal Census 1850: Washtenaw County (manuscript), p. 534.

23. Lithograph of Ann Arbor, 1853. Robert Burger.

Chapter 2
Page

24. Ann Arbor, 1856. Map of Washtenaw County, G.R. Bechler and E. Wenig.

26. "Opposition to Jews" notice. *Michigan Argus*, September 17, 1851, p. 3.

27. Ad for Henry Clay. *Michigan Argus*, May 16, 1856, p. 3.

29. Painting of Henry Philip Tappan.

31. Photograph of university buildings, late 1850s. *Michigan History*, Vol. 14 (1930), p. 576.

32. "Indignation Meeting" handbill.

33. Photograph of Union School, 1865.

38. Civil War recruiting poster.

41. "Queen Esther" handbill, 1866.

42. Handbill offering reward. Burton Historical Collection, Detroit Public Library.

43. Photographs of corner of Main and Washington streets, 1862 and 1869.

44. "Unparalleled Attraction" handbill, 1857.

45. "Town-Gown" cartoon. *University Palladium, 1874*, p. 103.

47. Photograph of Silas Douglas, c. 1860.

50. Photograph of Ann Arbor Organ Works, c. 1885.

51. Photograph of faculty and students in grass, c. 1876.

53. Photograph of man gazing at city from the northwest, 1876.

Chapter 3

Page

54. Panoramic View of Ann Arbor, 1880. Albert Ruger.

56. Photograph of University Hall under construction, 1872.

57. Bird's-eye view of campus, 1907.

59. "Fancy Goods" handbill, 1880s.

60. Photograph of Liberty Street looking west, c. 1870.

61. Photograph of Martin Vogel, c. 1885–1890.

62. "Maskenball" handbill, 1881.

63. Ad for Sam. B. Revenaugh. *University Palladium, 1874,* p. 111.

65. "Drunk Makers" handbill, 1881.

68. Ad for "The Two Sams." *Ann Arbor Courier,* April 30, 1884, p. 4

72. Photograph of Michigan Central Railroad Depot interior, 1890s. Burton Historical Collection, Detroit Public Library.

73. Photograph of Israel and Olivia Hall, late 1880s. Photograph of Junius Beal and family, 1890s.

75. Photograph of William Jennings Bryan at courthouse, October 11, 1900.

76. Photograph of Company A at courthouse, April 26, 1898.

78. "Gates of Mecca" post card.

80. Photograph of Fifth Ward school, 1908.

81. Photograph of Police Department, 1908.

82. "Riot Course" cartoon, 1908.

83. Photograph of workers in County Clerk's office, c. 1910.

84. Photograph of Allmendinger family, 1907.

85. Photograph of burned high school, 1905.

87. Photograph of Fire Department banquet, 1914. Photograph of Merchants Credit Association banquet, 1913. Photograph of the presidents of the Schwaebischen Unterstuetzung-Verein, 1888–1913.

89. Photograph of East Huron Street, c. 1910.

91. Photograph of Walker Livery, c. 1910.

Chapter 4

Page

92. Photograph of Main Street, c. 1914.

95. Ad for Martin Haller, *Daily Times-News,* December 24, 1917, p. 14.

96. Photograph of Ladies Aid Society, Zion Lutheran Church, April 12, 1917.

98. Photograph of July Fourth picnic, Zion Lutheran Church, c. 1914.

99. Photograph of Hoover Steel Ball Company, 1913. *The Evolution of the Steel Ball Industry* [1917?], p. 8. Drawing of Hoover Steel Ball Company, 1917. *The Evolution . . . Industry,* p. 11.

100. Photograph of Bartenders and Brewery Workers farewell banquet, April 21, 1918.

101. Photographs of military training. *Michiganensian 1919,* pp. 458, 461.

102. Housing notice. *Daily Times-News*, May 31, 1919, p. 8.

104. Ad for *Michigan Age. Ann Arbor Negro Year Book 1918–1919.*

106. Map of Burns Park. Olmstead Brothers, *Proposed Improvements for Ann Arbor,* 1922, p. 110.

107. Robert Frost article. *Ann Arbor Times-News*, February 16, 1922, p. 1.

109. Photograph of cars on State Street. *Ann Arbor Observer.*

111. Map of Ann Arbor. *Ann Arbor: The City Where Commerce and Education Meet,* 1925, Map A.

112. Photograph of the laying of the cornerstone of the Michigan League. *Ann Arbor Daily News,* March 30, 1928, p. 1.

114. Photograph of First National Bank Building. *Ann Arbor Daily News*, special edition, February 19, 1929, p. 1.

115. Ad for hotel project.

117. Photograph of State Street, c. 1927.

119. Work notice. Mayor's Unemployment Committee.

121. Photograph of Farmers' Market sheds under construction, 1940.

123. Photograph of Wendell Willkie at Michigan Central Railroad Depot, September 30, 1940. Courtesy of the Gandy Dancer restaurant.

124. My-T-Fine Cafe, South Thayer Street, c. 1930.

125. Photograph of central campus area near main library, c. 1940. Courtesy of Ivory Photo.

126. "An Open Letter," *Washtenaw Post-Tribune,* June 7, 1940, p. 3.

127. Can the Japs Bomb Michigan?" *Washtenaw Post-Tribune,* May 15, 1942, p. 6.

128. Photograph of mock battle at Ferry Field. *Ann Arbor News,* July 6, 1942, p. 12.

129. Ad for Fox Tent and Awning. *Washtenaw Post-Tribune,* August 14, 1942, p. 2.

130. Ad for Argus. *Washtenaw Post-Tribune,* May 19, 1944, p. 11.

131. Photograph of spectators watching Memorial Day parade. *Ann Arbor News,* May 31, 1945, p. 20.

133. Photograph of Ann Arbor from the west, 1939. *Ann Arbor News.*

Chapter 5
Page
134. Diagram of historical development, 1824–1960. *Ann Arbor 1960.*

137. Photograph of dedication of West Washington Street carport. *Ann Arbor News,* May 27, 1949, p. 28.

139. Cartoon of city drawing power. *Michigan Daily*, March 24, 1957.

140. Cartoon for new city charter.

143. Map of Urban Renewal area. A. D. Moore Papers, Bentley.

145. Photograph of subdivision, late 1950s. *Ann Arbor Observer.* Photograph of emerging County Building. *Ann Arbor News,* April 15, 1954, p. 30.

146. Photograph of couple on bridge.

147. Photograph of Lyndon Johnson walking to Michigan Stadium. *Ann Arbor News,* May 22, 1964, p. 13.

149. Photograph of Tower Plaza,

East William Street. *Ann Arbor Observer*.

151. Photograph of Fair Housing march around City Hall. *Ann Arbor News*, June 18, 1963, p. 11.

153. Reader referendum vote form. *Ann Arbor News*, April 5, 1970, p. 5.

154. Photograph of participants in Moratorium Day, 1969. *Ann Arbor News* , October 16, 1969, p. 1.

155. Photograph of "Student Strike Parade" along South State Street, November 5, 1968. Copyright Tom Copi.

156. Photograph of South University disturbances, June 1969. *Ann Arbor News*, June 19, 1969, p. 1.

158. Photograph of Arborland shopping center. *Ann Arbor News*, April 3, 1962, p. 3.

159. Handbill for Free Arts Festival, 1974.

160. Title page of *Ann Arbor Sun*, July 12, 1970, p. 1.

162. Photograph of Hash Bash, April 1, 1974. Courtesy of Eli Zaret.

164. Campaign poster for David Sinclair, spring elections 1973.

165. Election cartoon. *Ann Arbor News*, April 22, 1975, p. 19.

166. Photograph of sit-in protesters leaving First Presbyterian Church. *Ann Arbor News*, September 5, 1970, p. 10.

169. Photograph of Ann Arbor from the west, 1987. Peter Yates.

A Note on Sources

Primary sources for writing about the history of Ann Arbor are plentiful and readily available. Official city records and local newspapers reach back to the earliest days, as do census records (federal, state, and county) and a wealth of private papers. Many city records are to be found in the Michigan Historical Collections at the University of Michigan's Bentley Historical Library, including the papers of recent mayors; other legal and electoral records touching the city are held by the Washtenaw County Clerk. Several nineteenth-century censuses in manuscript are in the Bentley, while a complete run of the federal census is in the University of Michigan's Hatcher Graduate Library. The papers of scores of individuals, families, and organizations—churches, businesses, clubs, etc.—are also in the Bentley, which contains as well a rich collection of photographs and bound volumes of the city's nineteenth-century newspapers. Microfilm copies of these and their twentieth-century descendants are stored in the Hatcher Library.

Mention should also be made of the Ann Arbor Public Library's clipping file, covering the city's last twenty-five years, and of the Burton Collection in the Detroit Public Library, which includes many of John Allen's papers and other pertinent materials, including photographs. The records of the University of Michigan are deposited in the Bentley and necessarily contain much that is of immediate significance to the development of the city. Chief among these are the exhibition papers of the university regents, which expand considerably upon the published *Proceedings*, and the papers of hundreds of faculty and staff, notably those of the presidents. Letters and diaries of students also abound, and often they provide valuable insight into the city's life.

The secondary literature on Ann Arbor is not plentiful and often of limited value. The standard history, O. W. Stephenson's *Ann Arbor: The First Hundred Years* (1927), is out of date, unbalanced, and unreliable. Some of the chapters of *The Pictorial History of Ann Arbor 1824–1974* (1974) are helpful, but since each is short and written by a different person, the city's history is not seen whole. Lela Duff's *Pioneer School* (1958) and *Ann Arbor Yesterdays* (1962) have much interesting detail, as do Louis Doll's *A History of the Newspapers of Ann Arbor 1829–1920* (1959) and *The History of St. Thomas Parish, Ann Arbor* (1941). Several other churches have also had their histories compiled, but like Doll's book, these tend to be compendia of facts and names. The memoirs of Adam Christman, *Ann Arbor: The Changing Scene* (1984), and Milo Ryan, *View of a Universe: A Love Story of Ann Arbor at Middle Age* (1985), offer fond remembrances.

Scholarly articles on aspects of the city's history are also in short supply. Besides those cited in the notes, several others ought to be mentioned: W. Andrew Aschenbaum's "Toward Pluralism and Assimilation: The Religious Crisis of Ann Arbor's Wurttemberg Community," *Michigan History* 58 (1974); and David M. Katzman's "Ann Arbor: Depression City," *Michigan History* 50 (1966). Also of value are Helen Aminoff's "The First Jews of Ann Arbor," *Michigan Jewish History* 23 (1983), and John M. Burgess's unpublished master's thesis, "A Study of the Negro in Ann Arbor, Michigan" (1932), which is in the Bentley. Much more has been written about the university, and the best place to begin looking for information relating to the city is the *Encyclopedic Survey* (1942–1981).

NOTES

I have cited sources only for quotations not already identified. These are keyed to the text by page number and first word(s).

Chapter 1

Page

1. **"without any regard"**: Julius P.B. MacCabe, "Notes on the Village of Ann Arbor," *Detroit Daily Advertiser*, September 12, 1848, p. 3.

2. **"cause a true"**: *Laws of the Territory of Michigan* (1871-84), Vol. 1, p. 816.

   "the amount" and ff.: Russell E. Bidlack, "John Allen and the Founding of Ann Arbor" (1962), p. 13.

   "several": Ezra Maynard to William S. Maynard, June 5, 1824. Maynard Papers, Bentley.

   "on the most": Bidlack, p. 16.

3. **"Our water"** and ff.: John Allen to Jane Trimble, February 20, 1825. Allen Papers, Bentley.

4. **"rich as"** and ff.: Lucy Morgan to family, July 13, 1831. Morgan Papers, Bentley.

5. **"like a prince"**: "Karl Neidhard's Reise nach Michigan," *Michigan History*, 35 (1951), p. 64.

6. **"something higher"**: George Corselius, Diary, August 7, 1833. Bentley.

   "I have been": Corselius, February 25, 1838.

   " the ladies": Corselius,

August 13, 1833.

   "their patriarch": "Neidhard's Reise," p. 47.

7. **"There is"** and ff.: Friedrich Schmid to Basel Mission, August 27, 1833. *The Schmid Letters*, translated by Emerson J. Hutzel (1953), p. 9.

8. **"to do all things"**: *Laws of the Territory of Michigan*, Vol. 3, p. 1210.

   "the whole": *Michigan Argus*, June 11, 1845, p. 2.

   "that dreaded": *Michigan Argus*, November 13, 1850, p. 2.

10. **"secure the shadow"**: *Michigan Argus*, September 25, 1844, p. 2.

    "run over": Ann Arbor Council Minutes, August 24, 1839.

11. **"some of the curtains"** and ff.: *Michigan Argus*, March 25, 1838, p. 2.

    "delirium tremens": Notes by Benjamin Packard, Stewart Papers, Burton Historical Collection, Detroit Public Library.

    "showing": *Michigan Argus*, October 9, 1844, p. 3.

    "Black List": Council Minutes, June 14, 1847. The actual expression was not used until May 12, 1849.

13. **"speculation"**: *State Journal*, April 13, 1837, p. 2.

15. **"Our enterprising"**: *State Journal*, March 23, 1837, p. 2.

"raw . . . settlement" and ff.: Harriet Martineau, *Society in America* (1837), Vol. 1, p. 319.

"Too long": *State Journal*, September 24, 1835, p. 3.

"our midst": *Michigan Argus*, January 10, 1849, p. 2.

18. **"Do we find"**: *Michigan Argus*, March 25, 1846, p. 2.

"into the right": M. Howard to William Woodbridge, July 8, 1844. Cited in Ronald P. Formisano, *The Birth of Mass Political Parties: Michigan, 1827-1861* (1971), p. 199, n. 10.

"All such": *Articles of the Native American Association of Ann Arbor*, Bentley.

19. **"boys from 5-16"**: *State Journal*, September 24, 1835, p. 3.

"as soon as": *Michigan Argus*, October 28, 1846, p. 3.

"Those diseases": Federal Census 1850: Washtenaw County (manuscript), p. 611.

"to disarm": *Michigan Argus*, May 23, 1849, p. 2.

"our village": *Michigan Argus*, October 28, 1846, p. 2.

21. **"We who have"**: Henry P. Tappan, *A Discourse delivered . . . on the occasion of his Inauguration as Chancellor* (1852), p. 4.

"illuminated balloons" and ff.: *Michigan Argus*, July 10, 1850, p. 2.

"worldly pursuits": *Michigan Argus*, June 26, 1850, p. 2.

"surviving heroes" and ff.: *Michigan Argus*, July 10, 1850, p. 2.

22. **"among strangers"**: *Michigan Argus*, April 30, 1851, p. 2.

"an efficient": *Washtenaw Whig*, February 19, 1851, p. 2.

"to organize": *Acts of the Legislature 1851*, p. 125.

"the detection": *Michigan Argus*, June 25, 1845, p. 2.

"second town": *Washtenaw Whig*, February 19, 1851, p. 2.

"three hearty cheers" and ff.: *Washtenaw Whig*, April 9, 1851, p. 2.

"the Recorder": Council Minutes, April 9, 1851.

Chapter 2
Page

28. **"mechanical arts"**: *Minutes of the State Convention of the Colored Citizens of the State of Michigan (1843), p. 11.*

"now commences": *Michigan State News*, February 26, 1861, p. 1.

"a new Athens" and ff.: Tappan, *A Discourse*, pp. 51–52.

30. **"objectionable"**: *President's Report to the Board of Regents, 1853*, p. 12.

"board and rooming": *Regents Proceedings 1837–1864*, p. 646.

"desiring to take": *Local News and Advertiser*, September 14, 1858, p. 2.

"vast and vital": Tappan, *A Discourse*, p. 9.

"Nothing would": *Washtenaw Whig*, January 5, 1853, p. 2.

"make some": *President's Report . . . 1853*, p. 11.

"Detroit gentlemen," and ff.: *Local News and Advertiser*, March 20, 1860, p. 2.

"assurances": *Regents Proceedings 1837–1864*, p. 915.

"reason to believe": *Ibid.*, p. 956.

"removal": *Local News and Advertiser*, April 3, 1860, p. 2.

31. "ornament": *Washtenaw Whig*, July 9, 1851, p. 2.

   "Our city": *Michigan Argus*, November 24, 1854, p. 2.

   "able and learned": *Michigan Argus*, January 10, 1849, p. 2.

32. "large and crowded" and ff.: *Washtenaw Whig*, January 2, 1850, p. 1.

33. "too great": *Washtenaw Whig*, May 10, 1854, p. 2.

   "welfare": *Local News and Advertiser*, December 28, 1858, p. 2.

34. "foreign scholars": *Washtenaw Whig*, January 18, 1854, p. 2.

   "People are beginning": *Local News and Advertiser*, September 28, 1858, p. 2.

   "either we must": *Local News and Advertiser*, July 27, 1858, p. 2.

   "in almost": *Ann Arbor Journal*, September 5, 1855, p. 2.

35. "Our city": *Local News and Advertiser*, August 31, 1858, p. 2.

   "stretching": *Michigan Argus*, May 20, 1859, p. 3.

"by any inland": *Local News and Advertiser*, July 21, 1857, p. 2.

"were much pleased": Lela Duff, *Pioneer School* (1958), p. 13.

36. "nationality": *Michigan Argus*, April 10, 1868, p. 3.

   "services . . . to": *Ann Arbor Journal*, January 16, 1861. Cited in George S. May, "Ann Arbor and the Coming of the Civil War," *Michigan History*, 36 (1952), p. 244.

37. "the families of": *Michigan Argus*, May 3, 1861, p. 2.

   "extend aid": *Michigan Argus*, July 17, 1863, p. 2.

   "still strewed": *Michigan Argus*, August 7, 1863, p. 2.

38. "Festival" and ff.: *Michigan Argus*, December 11, 1863, p. 3.

39. "as zealous": *Ann Arbor Journal*, August 13, 1862, p. 2.

   "principal cities": *Michigan Argus*, October 28, 1864, p. 3.

   "it might be": *Michigan Argus*, January 1, 1864, p. 2.

   "languishing": *Michigan Argus*, July 3, 1863, p. 2.

40. "Many of" and ff.: Erastus O. Haven, *Autobiography*, edited by C. C. Stratton (1883), p. 143.

   "property . . . changing": *Michigan Argus*, April 15, 1864, p. 3.

   "Will not": *Michigan Argus*, July 28, 1865, p. 3.

   "There are": *Michigan Argus*, September 15, 1865, p. 3.

"I had to pay": Comments of Hugh B. Alexander in a letter of October 19, 1865. "College Days in Ann Arbor: 1865–1868," *Michigan History*, 37 (1953), p. 327.

42. **"white folks"**: *Michigan Argus*, January 9, 1863, p. 3.

   "we no longer": *Peninsular Courier*, November 11, 1870, p. 2.

   "machines": *Michigan Argus*, April 14, 1865, p. 3.

43. **"Queen"**: Julia Silk, *The Campaign of Mrs. Julia Silk* (1892), p. 40.

   "an orderly": *Michigan Argus*, February 15, 1867, p. 2.

44. **"high prices"**: Erastus O. Haven to E. C. Walker, August 9, 1864. Walker Papers, Bentley.

46. **"people throughout"** and ff.: *Michigan Argus*, April 3, 1863, p. 2.

   "disgraced": *Michigan Argus*, April 19, 1867, p. 1.

   "rigidly enforced": *Peninsular Courier*, June 11, 1869, p. 3.

   "quite a revival": *Peninsular Courier*, March 25, 1870, p. 3.

47. **"alarmingly"**: *Peninsular Courier*, June 11, 1869, p. 3.

   "but a victory": *Peninsular Courier*, April 7, 1871, p. 2.

   "every place": *Peninsular Courier*, June 2, 1871, p. 3.

48. **"These sources"** and ff.: Council Minutes, October 24, 1871.

"interests": Handbill announcing Taxpayers' Meeting, Council Minutes, May 17, 1875.

   "Its large": *Michigan Argus*, February 26, 1864, p. 2.

   "welfare": *Michigan Argus*, August 18, 1865, p. 3.

   "gratifying": *Regents Proceedings 1864–1870*, p. 57.

49. **"simply because"**: *Peninsular Courier*, July 14, 1871, p. 3.

   "the Lowell": *Peninsular Courier*, April 28, 1871, p. 2.

   "if it were not": *Peninsular Courier*, October 1, 1875, p. 3.

   "dwindle": *Peninsular Courier*, December 11, 1874, p. 3.

50. **"there is no"**: *Peninsular Courier*, July 5, 1872, p. 3.

   "as much": *Peninsular Courier*, July 7, 1871, p. 3.

   "mammoth": *Peninsular Courier*, May 23, 1873, p. 3.

   "a manufacturing place" and ff.: *Peninsular Courier*, January 21, 1876, p. 3.

52. **"an air"** and ff.: *New York Daily Graphic*, June 7, 1878, p. 693.

   "honorable pioneers": *Ann Arbor Courier*, August 23, 1878, p. 3.

Chapter 3
Page

55. **"not only"** and ff.: *Ann Arbor Courier*, October 8, 1880, p. 3.

56. **"one of the finest"**: *Ann Arbor Courier*, February 20, 1880, p. 3.

"once again" and ff.: *Ann Arbor Courier*, September 3, 1880, p. 3.

57. "patronized": *Ann Arbor Courier*, February 9, 1887 p. 2.
"alive": *Ann Arbor Courier*, July 15, 1881, p. 3.

58. "a miniature": *Ann Arbor Courier*, July 2, 1880, p. 3.
"lethargy": *Ann Arbor Courier*, July 15, 1881, p. 3.
"a certain class": *Ann Arbor Democrat (Supplement)*, April 10, 1879.
"large" and ff.: *Ann Arbor Courier*, April 25, 1879, p. 3.

61. "poor boy": *Peninsular Courier*, June 13, 1873, p. 3.

62. "wounded": *Peninsular Courier*, September 16, 1870, p. 3.

64. "bigger than": *Peninsular Courier*, June 7, 1872, p. 2.
"to take the" *Ann Arbor Courier*, March 18, 1881, p. 2.

66. "to quench": *Ann Arbor Courier*, April 6, 1887, p. 3.
"There was only": *Ann Arbor Courier*, April 6, 1883, p. 3.
"and generally": *Citizens League of Ann Arbor* (1884), p. 24. Bentley.

67. "In Ann Arbor" and ff.: *Ann Arbor Courier*, February 20, 1889, p. 2.
"given to our care": *Ann Arbor Courier*, May 5, 1886, p. 2.
"should put": *Ann Arbor Register*, February 14, 1884, p. 2.
"There isn't": *Ann Arbor Courier*, March 18, 1885, p. 2.

69. "the tendency": *Ann Arbor Courier*, February 17, 1886, p. 2.
"common people": *Ann Arbor Courier*, July 28, 1886, p. 3.
"the class": *Ann Arbor Courier*, January 27, 1886, p. 2.
"We should not": *Ann Arbor Courier*, August 24, 1887, p. 2.
"the element" and ff.: *Ann Arbor Courier*, December 14, 1887, p. 2.
"educational center": *Ann Arbor Courier*, August 24, 1887, p. 2.
"boodle fund": *Ann Arbor Courier*, November 2, 1887, p. 2.
"chief ones": *Ann Arbor Register*, August 25, 1887, p. 5.

71. "alderman at large" and ff.: Samuel W. Beakes, *Past and Present of Washtenaw County* (1906), p. 704.
"have been running": *Ann Arbor Register*, April 19, 1894, p. 4.

72. "The improved": *Communication from the Board of Public Works* (1896), p. 2.

74. "to the city": *Ann Arbor Courier*, June 12, 1889, p. 3.
"Never have": *Ann Arbor Courier*, September 24, 1890, p. 3.
"always takes" Emily Jane Hollister, Diary, July 27, 1891. Bentley.

75. "hostile feelings": *Ann Arbor Courier*, November 19, 1890, p. 2.

"**I shall be glad**" and ff.: *Ann Arbor Courier Register*, October 17, 1900, p. 2.

76. "**Two thousand students**": *Ann Arbor Courier*, March 30, 1898, p. 1.

"**holiday soldiers**": *Ann Arbor Courier*, April 7, 1898, p. 1.

77. "**as a memento**": Council Minutes, May 10, 1899.

"**That they**": *Ann Arbor Daily Argus*, May 19, 1899, p. 2.

"**home establishments**": *Ann Arbor Courier*, December 5, 1894, p. 2.

"**be found**": *Ann Arbor and Ypsilanti Directory 1892*, unpaginated description of city.

78. "**out of men**": *The University of Michigan: An Encyclopedic Survey*, edited by Wilfred B. Shaw et al. (1942–1981), Vol. 1, p. 71.

"**never before**": *Regents Proceedings 1901–1906*, p. 224.

"**Never before**": *Ann Arbor Courier Register*, May 14, 1902, p. 1.

80. "**Hugh**": *Ann Arbor Michigan 1905-6*, p. 12. Burton Historical Collection, Detroit Public Library.

"**respectfully petitioned**": Petition to Royal Copeland from S. Simmons and 36 others [1901]. Copeland Papers, Bentley.

"**believing that**": petition to Royal Copeland from Hermann Krapf and 36 others [1901]. Copeland Papers, Bentley.

81. "**metropolitan style**": *Ann Arbor Courier*, May 15, 1907, p. 1.

"**Gentlemen**": Shirley W. Smith, *Harry Burns Hutchins and the University of Michigan* (1951), p. 101.

83. "**Ann Arbor people**": *Daily Times-News*, July 18, 1910, p. 1.

"**manufacturing interests**": *Ann Arbor News, Times, and Argus*, May 8, 1908, p. 4.

84. "**ordinary factory town**": *Ann Arbor Courier Register*, August 13, 1902, p. 6.

"**a residence place**": *Daily Times-News*, May 8, 1909, p. 8.

85. "**done great things**": *Year Book, Ann Arbor Civic Association* (1914), p. 2. Bentley.

86. "**objectionable resorts**": "Resolutions of Social Purity Club." Wilgus Papers, Bentley.

"**supervision**" and ff.: *Daily Times-News*, October 19, 1911, p. 5.

"**either unoccupied**": *Daily Times-News*, April 4, 1913, p. 1.

"**city of residences**": *Daily Times-News*, January 29, 1913, p. 3.

"**this most deadly**" and ff.: *Year Book, Ann Arbor Civic Association* (1914), p. 26. Bentley.

88. "**willing and anxious**" and ff.: *Daily Times-News*, April 22, 1914, p. 1.

"**for the sole use**": Council Minutes, August 4, 1913.

"**people who**": *Daily Times-News*, April 22, 1914, p. 1.

"none had" and ff.: *Daily Times-News*, April 2, 1914, p. 1.

89. "frat man": *Daily Times-News*, March 25, 1914, p. 4.

90. "Speeders": *Daily Times-News*, September 7, 1911, p. 1.

Chapter 4
Page

93. "most dreadful": *Daily Times-News*, August 1, 1914, p. 3.

94. "a banner year": *Daily Times-News*, January 3, 1916, p. 1.
"Practically": *Daily Times-News*, December 30, 1916, p. 1.
"Ann Arbor Girls": *Detroit Labor News*, December 22, 1916, p. 1.
"much better": *Daily Times-News*, November 25, 1916, p. 1.
"I don't" and ff.: *Daily Times-News*, December 19, 1916, p. 1.
"exorbitant": *Daily Times-News*, December 15, 1916, p. 3.

95. "happy voices": *Daily Times-News*, December 24, 1917, p. 2.

96. "allegiance": *Daily Times-News*, April 5, 1914, p. 3.
"indifference": *Daily Times-News*, April 6, 1918, p. 2.

97. "war had gotten": *Daily Times-News*, October 9, 1917, p. 10.
"We feel": *Washtenaw Post*, January 3, 1918, p. 1.
"elections": *Regents Proceedings 1917-1920*, p. 190.
"the excuse": Claud Van Tyne to Frederick Paxon, April

12, 1918. Cited in James D. Wilkes, "Van Tyne: The Professor and the Hun," *Michigan History*, 55 (1971), p. 190.
"You are either": Howard H. Peckham, *The Making of the University of Michigan* (1967), p. 130.
"Many persons": *Washtenaw Post*, May 2, 1918, p. 1.

98. "disgraceful episode": *Daily Times-News*, April 16, 1918, p. 3.
"little colonies": *Daily Times-News*, March 21, 1918, p. 4.
"to oppose German": *Washtenaw Post*, April 11, 1918, p. 6.
"by a vote": *Daily Times-News*, September 10, 1918, p. 1.

100. "Greek boy": Pearl Ahnen & Mary Hunt, "The Greeks in Ann Arbor," *Ann Arbor Observer*, April 1986, p. 51.
"foreigners": *Daily Times-News*, December 15, 1916, p. 1.

103. "send mail orders": *Souvenir Program*, Labor Day, September 2, 1901, p. 13.
"more money": *Ann Arbor Times-News*, December 31, 1919, p. 1.
"a record": *Ann Arbor Negro Year Book, 1917–1918*, p. 2.

105. "Only twelve per cent": *Ann Arbor: The City Where Commerce and Education Meet* (1925), unpaginated. Bentley.
"a plan by": *Daily Times-News*, February 17, 1914, p. 3.
"having interests": Olmsted

Brothers, *Proposed Improvements for Ann Arbor*, 1922, p. 1. Bentley.

"for the heavy": *Ibid.*, p. 45.

106. "large amount": *Ibid.*, p. 44.

"growing volume": *Ibid.*, p. 22.

"with a courageous": *Ibid.*, p. ii.

107. "for granted": *Ann Arbor Times-News*, February 14, 1922, p. 1.

"even more attractive": *Ann Arbor Times-News*, February 11, 1922, p. 4.

108. "We first": *President's Report for the Year 1921-1922*, p. 10.

"outside property": *Ann Arbor Times-News*, February 11, 1922, p. 1.

"It will mean": *Ann Arbor Times-News*, February 15, 1922, p. 1.

110. "exceptional": *Regents Proceedings 1926–1929*, p. 244.

"sent broadcast": C. J. Hutzel, "Past History of Ann Arbor Chamber of Commerce" (1927). Chamber of Commerce Papers, Bentley.

"Ann Arbor is" and ff.: *Ann Arbor: The City Where Commerce and Education Meet*, unpaginated. Bentley.

111. "the right kind": *Ann Arbor Daily News*, March 21, 1930, p. 4.

"a pleasant seat": Edward Staebler to council, April 18, 1927. Staebler Papers, Bentley.

"Ann Arbor firms": Shirley

Smith to Edward Staebler, November 28, 1930. Staebler Papers, Bentley.

112. "the industry": *Ann Arbor Times-News*, February 1, 1922, p. 5.

"one of the greatest": *Ann Arbor Times-News*, July 5, 1924, p. 1.

113. "a citizen army": *Detroit Times*, November 21, 1928, p. 1.

"I call it": *Washtenaw Tribune*, January 8, 1929, p. 1.

"breach of faith": *Detroit Times*, November 21, 1928, p. 16.

"the business interests": *Washtenaw Tribune*, November 28, 1928, p. 1.

"determined to divorce": *Detroit Times*, November 21, 1928, p. 1.

"situations" and ff.: *Regents Proceedings 1926–1929*, p. 876.

"regret": *Ibid.*, p. 864.

114. "best hotels": Brochure for Citizens Hotel Company. Chamber of Commerce Papers, Bentley.

116. "urgent necessities": Edward Staebler to L. M. Hollis, January 14, 1931. Staebler Papers, Bentley.

"one great park": *Labor Review* (1929), p. 11. Published by Ann Arbor Trades Council.

"like Charlie": *Ann Arbor Times-News*, April 5, 1921, p. 4.

117. "Surely Ann Arbor": O. W. Stephenson, *Ann Arbor: The First*

Hundred Years (1927), p. 432.

118. **"ten year problem"**: Edward Staebler to State Committee on Employment, March 21, 1931. Staebler Papers, Bentley.

120. **"verge of hunger"**: *Ibid.*
"the financial structures": *Report of the Mayors Conference, May 18, 1932*, p. 1.
"hanging on": *Ann Arbor Tribune*, March 31, 1933, p. 1.

121. **"no bridges"**: *Ann Arbor Tribune*, April 6, 1933, p. 1.
"largely due": Printed speech, dated January 10, 1931. Newkirk Papers, Bentley.

122. **"every possible"**: Greg Wolper, "The New Deal in Ann Arbor," student thesis, 1982, p. 26. Bentley.
"pre-depression": *Ann Arbor Daily News*, January 1, 1936, p. 4.

123. **"driest"**: *Ann Arbor Daily News*, April 11, 1933, p. 1.
"main issue": *Ann Arbor News*, November 4, 1940, p. 4.
"the gates": *Ann Arbor News*, October 30, 1940, p. 4.

126. **"Certain vicious"**: *Washtenaw Post-Tribune*, June 7, 1940, p. 7.
"unthinkingly": *Washtenaw Post-Tribune*, June 14, 1940, p. 7.

127. **"in the event:"** *Washtenaw Post-Tribune*, December 19, 1941, p. 1.

128. **"methods of self-defense"**: *Washtenaw Post-Tribune*, April 3, 1942, p. 1.

"We expect": *Washtenaw Post-Tribune*, June 5, 1942, p. 1.

129. **"is too sweet"**: *Washtenaw Post-Tribune*, August 4, 1942, p. 7.

130. **"stripped"**: *Washtenaw Post-Tribune*, December 25, 1942, p. 1.

131. **"they did not know"**: *Washtenaw Post-Tribune*, February 4, 1944, p. 1.

132. **"old established"**: *Washtenaw Post-Tribune*, October 8, 1943, p. 1.

Chapter 5
Page

136. **"Whatever . . . is available"**: Walter C. Sadler to William E. Brown, January 25, 1946. Brown Papers, Bentley.
"Practically all": Edith M. Bader to William E. Brown, February 14, 1946. Brown Papers, Bentley.
"start a project": William E. Brown to Metropolitan Life Insurance Company, September 5, 1947. Brown Papers, Bentley.
"perfect deal": *Ann Arbor News*, October 25, 1946, p. 1.
"ridiculously low": *Ann Arbor News*, March 18, 1947, p. 3.

137. **"making the traffic"**: William E. Brown to Philip T. Shanks, October 22, 1947. Brown Papers, Bentley.
"to run this city": *Washtenaw Post-Tribune*, February 9, 1945, p. 1.

"thankless": *Washtenaw Post-Tribune*, June 15, 1945, p. 6.

138. **"deteriorated"**: William E. Brown to Otis Hardy, October 23, 1945. Brown Papers, Bentley.

    "of the right type": *Washtenaw Post-Tribune*, February 9, 1945, p. 1.

    "champion": *Detroit News*, April 3, 1957, p. 58.

141. **"sacred document"**: William E. Brown to Charter Commission, January 26, 1954. Charter Commission Papers, Bentley.

    "piecemeal" and ff.: *Ann Arbor News*, March 10, 1954, p. 17.

    "neither endorsing": *Ann Arbor News*, March 25, 1955, p. 15.

    "that communist" and ff.: *Detroit Free Press*, March 26, 1955, p. 1.

    "every moral" and ff.: Albert Wheeler to Charter Commission, January 26, 1954. Charter Commission Papers, Bentley.

142. **"normal channels"**: Henry Lewis to Samuel J. Eldersveld, February 10, 1959. Eldersveld Papers, Bentley.

144. **"morally wrong"**: *Ann Arbor News*, June 11, 1959, p. 23.

    "because it is socialistic": George Wedemeyer, in a talk to Kiwanis Club, November 17, 1958. Creal Papers, Bentley.

147. **"to end poverty"**: *Ann Arbor News*, May 22, 1964, p. 1.

    "I am delighted": Tape of John F. Kennedy speech in Ann Arbor, October 14, 1960. Bentley.

148. **"smiled a cheery"**: *Ann Arbor Daily News*, October 3, 1932, p. 1.

    "going its way" and ff.: *Detroit Free Press*, September 10, 1962, p. D-10.

    "the Michigan": Tape of Kennedy speech. Bentley.

151. **"race, creed"**: Council Minutes, March 5, 1962.

    "grossly inadequate": *Ann Arbor News*, August 3, 1963, p. 11.

152. **"model"** and ff.: *Ann Arbor News*, March 23, 1967, p. 1.

    "people" and ff.: *Official Entry . . . All-America City Award*, September 30, 1966. Bentley.

154. **"agony"**: *Ann Arbor News*, October 16, 1969, p. 25.

155. **"mismanagement"**: *Detroit Free Press*, June 20, 1969, p. A-6.

156. **"move out"**: Memo to Mayor Robert J. Harris from his secretary, June 17, 1969. Harris Papers, Bentley.

157. **"from a small"**: *General Characteristics of Population and Housing in 1970*, p. 1.

    "engrained": *Ann Arbor News*, October 13, 1970, p. 15.

158. **"Does growth"** and ff.: *Ann Arbor News*, October 23, 1970, p. 15.

160. **"Now the students"**: *Michigan Daily*, January 25, 1967, p. 4.

161. **"people and ecology"**: Anthony Ralph Smith, "College Town Radicals: The Case of the Ann Arbor Human Rights Party," University of Illinois doctoral dissertation (1980), p. 183.

165. **"I am opposed"**: *Ann Arbor News*, August 22, 1974, p. 35.

"being taken": Anthony Ralph Smith, p. 236.

166. **"raising hell"**: "Albert Wheeler Remembers: Part Two," *Ann Arbor Observer*, October 1976, p. 6.

167. **"Oh, it was"**: *Detroit Free Press*, March 7, 1976, p. A-3.

INDEX

abolitionism, 28, 161

Afro-American Liberty Club, 103

agriculture, Washtenaw County, 3, 16

Allen, Ann, 6

Allen, J. Adams, 33

Allen, John, 1-2, 3, 5, 8, 10, 15, 22, 23, 28, 106, 117, 167

Allen's Creek, 3, 23, 25

Allmendinger, G.F., 84, 86

American Broach and Machine Co., 122–123

Angell, James B., 56–57, 78, 79, 81, 93

Angell Hall, 108

Ann Arbor: All-America city, 152; boundaries, 18, 24, 25, 74, 109, 135, 138, 157; centennial, 116–117; founding, 1–2; incorporation as city (1851), 23; incorporation as village (1833), 7–8; names, 2; 75th anniversary, 77; sesquicentennial, 166; state capital bid, 13

Ann Arbor Agricultural Works, 58

Ann Arbor American, 18

Ann Arbor Argus, 71, 77

Ann Arbor Bar, 30

Ann Arbor Board of Realtors, 144

Ann Arbor Civic Association, 85–88, 94, 105–106, 116, 165

Ann Arbor Civic Forum, 141–142

Ann Arbor Courier, 52, 56, 66, 69, 70, 74

Ann Arbor Daily News, 121, 122, 123

"Ann Arbor Days," 94

Ann Arbor Fair Housing Association, 151

Ann Arbor High School, see Union School

Ann Arbor Land Co., 13–16, 23, 68

Ann Arbor National Defense Committee, 126

Ann Arbor Negro Year Book, 103, 105

Ann Arbor News, 127

Ann Arbor Times-News, 106

Ann Arbor Register, 67

anti-German sentiment, see prejudice

anti-Jewish sentiment, see prejudice

Argus Camera, 122

Asians, 142, 150

automobiles, see industry and commerce; transportation

Bach, Philip, 35, 36, 43

Barrett, L.A., 98

Barry Guards, 37

Beakes, Samuel W., 71, 84

Beal, Junius, 70, 73, 74, 79, 88, 113

Berry, John, 7

Bethel A.M.E. Church, 55, 98

Bethlehem Evangelical Church, 88–89

Bethlehem Evangelical parochial school, 63

Birney, James, 28

birth control clinic, 86

Bismarck, Otto von, 88–89, 147

Black Action Movement, 152

Black Economic Development League, 166–167

Blackburn, William, 80–81

blacks: activism (see also civil rights movement), 27, 80–81, 103–105, 132, 141–142, 166–167; community role, 27–28, 41–42, 79–80, 103–105, 109, 124, 142, 144, 150; and Depression, 118; in police department, 80–81; university enrollment of, 28, 41, 150

Blair, Austin, 37

Board of Commerce, 83–85

boosterism, 11–15, 19, 35, 55, 67–70, 80, 85–88, 94, 110, 116–117, 150

Briarwood, 157, 167

Brook, James, 27
Brown, Anson, 5-6
Brown, Claude, 105
Brown, William E., 132, 136-138, 141, 146, 162
Bryan, William Jennings, 75-76
Burger, Robert, 23
Burns, George P., 88
Burton, Marion L. 108, 112
business college, 43
Businessman's Association of Ann Arbor, 69-70

Campbell, Robert, 122
Canadian settlement, 16
Carpenter, C.W., 144
cemeteries: Forest Hill, 35, 52, 90; Jewish, 26, 49
census, county: 1827, 3; 1845, 18
census, state: 1854, 21; 1874, 49, 58
census, federal: 1840, 3; 1850, 7, 18-19, 20-21; 1860, 21, 36; 1870, 40, 41, 49, 135; 1880, 58, 63; 1890, 74; 1900, 74, 83; 1910, 83, 100, 103; 1930, 109; 1940, 122, 124, 135, 150; 1950, 144; 1960, 144, 150; 1970, 149, 150, 157; 1980, 167
churches, religious organizations, 72; Council of Churches, 144; see also individual church names
citizen boards, 71, 141
Citizens Association for Area Planning, 158
Citizens for Good Housing, 163
Citizens League, 66-67
city charters, 18, 23, 70-71, 116, 140-141
city plan, 1-2, 11-13, 55
city planning, 105-107, 158
city-university relations (see also U-M students, conduct off-campus), 13, 30-33, 39-40, 48, 79, 108, 113-114, 132, 136-137, 140, 148
City Poor Committee, 120
civil rights movement (see also black

activism), 42, 141-142, 150-152
Civil War, 36-43
Clay, Henry (black laborer), 20, 27-28, 44
Clements (Wm. L.) Library, 108
Cleveland, Grover, 117
Colored Citizens of Michigan, convention, 27
commerce, see industry and commerce
Committee on Industry and Labor, 86
communications: telegraph, 19; telephone, 64, 70
Community Fund, 119
Congregational Church, 88, 98
conscription (Civil War), 38
Copeland, Royal, 80
Corselius, George, 6, 10, 11, 15, 22, 37
Corselius, William, 37
County Building, 144-146
county courthouses, 4, 15, 48, 93
county seat, 2-4
Crawford, Katherine, 79
Creal, Cecil, 144, 146
crime, 23, 44, 81, 101
Cullen, Thomas, 7
culture, cultural organizations (see also music), 6, 10, 15, 16, 31, 35
Currier, Nathaniel, 11

Daily Times-News, 83, 89, 94, 100, 101, 105
Darling, Cyrenus, 71
Davidson, John, 41
Dean, Henry S., 70
debating clubs, 3, 6, 15
Democrats (see also politics), 36, 42, 66, 80, 117, 129, 138, 151, 153, 161, 165
Depression, see economy
Detroit, impact on Ann Arbor's development, 13, 58, 77, 103, 167
Detroit Gazette, 2
Detroit Labor News, 94
development (see also university

growth and expansion; urban renewal), 34, 43, 56–58, 72, 73, 79, 109, 112, 114–115, 140, 144–145, 148–150, 157–158, 167
Douglas, Lloyd C., 98
Douglas, Silas, 37, 47–48, 71
"dry island," 66, 123, 150
"Dutch War," 45

East Ann Arbor, 138
Eberbach, Christian, 36, 63, 77
economy (see also development; industry and commerce), 18, 34–36, 49–50, 56–58, 67–71, 77, 83–86, 94–95, 103, 108–109, 111–115, 117–124, 138–140; depression (1893), 71; Depression (1930s), 113, 117–122; Panic of 1837, 18; Panic of 1873, 49–50
Eggert, Carl, 97
Eisenhower, Dwight D., 146
Eldersveld, Samuel J., 142, 144, 161
elections, local: 1833, 8; 1850s, 23, 25, 36; 1860s, 36, 37, 48; 1871, 47; 1880s, 66, 69; 1890s, 37, 71; 1905, 85; 1913, 85; 1920s, 109, 116; 1930s, 121, 123; 1940s, 131, 132; 1950s, 138, 141; 1960s, 161, 163; 1970s, 161–163, 165
elections, state: 1870, 42; 1874, 60; 1887, 65–66; 1916, 100–101; 1926, 146; 1936, 123; 1940, 146
elections, national: 1840s, 18, 28; 1860, 36; 1900, 75–76; 1912, 117; 1928, 117; 1932, 117; 1936, 123; 1940, 123–124; 1950s, 146; 1960s, 146, 161; 1972, 163
Emigrants' Guide to the State Of Michigan, 7
Employment Bureau, 119–121
Engels, Friedrich, 121

fair housing ordinance, 150–152, 163
Family Welfare Bureau, 119
Fantle, Charles, 26

Farmers' Market, 121
Felch, Alpheus, 48
Fierle, William, 62
Figle, Christena, 21
fire and fire protection, 8–10, 64, 137, 163
First Congregational Church, 98
First Methodist Church, 46, 146
Forest Hill Cemetery, 35, 52, 90
Forsyth, L.L., 96
Free Soil Party, 28
Freeman, John, 27
Freeman, Thomas, 27, 28
Friends of Labor, 103
Frieze, Henry Simmons, 34
Frost, Robert, at U-M, 107
Fuller, Edward, 18

Garfield, James A., 34
German community, 6–7, 17, 18, 36, 40, 60–64, 66, 74, 88–89; 1914–1918, 94–99; 1920s, 105; 1940s, 124, 126–127
Goldwater, Barry, 161
Graduate Employees Organization (U-M), 152
Graf, Ernest, 101
Greater Ann Arbor Research Park, 140
Greek community, 99–100
Green, Fred W., 113
Guiteau, Charles, 34
Guiterman, Simon, 27

Hall, Israel and Olivia, 73
Hall, Louis P., 95
Hangsterfer, Jacob, 35
Hargo, Franklin, 41
Harmon, Tom, 131
Harra, Lana, 20
Harris, Robert J., 155–157, 161–162
Harvey, Douglas, 155
hash bash, see marijuana ordinance
Haskins, Barry, 7
Haven, Erastus O., 40, 44, 46, 48

Helber, Eugene, 96, 97
Helber James, 97
Henderson, John C., 81
Hill, George D., 35
Hill Auditorium, 79, 89
Hiscock, Maria, 77
Hobbs, William, 97, 126
holiday celebrations: Christmas, 95,
    130; July 4th, 22, 35, 52, 58, 116,
    128; Memorial Day, 131;
    Washington's Birthday, 27, 35
Home Front Cues, 128
Hoover, Herbert, 117
Hoover Steel Ball Company, 83, 94,
    99, 100, 103, 115, 124
hospitals: homeopathic, 73–74, 79;
    university, 31, 48, 88, 108, 136;
    VA, 138, 140
Housewives League of Ann Arbor,
    94–95
housing (see also civil rights move-
    ment; urban renewal), 157; costs,
    rents, 40, 44, 69, 108, 163; short-
    ages, 41, 44, 102, 129–130,
    135–136; student housing, see U-M
    students
Housing Commission, 151–152
Human Relations Commission, 142,
    151
Human Rights Party, 161–166
human services, 10, 71, 119–121
Humphrey, Hubert, 161
Huron River, 1, 2, 3, 5, 7, 11, 13, 23,
    28, 142, 167
Huron River Manufacturing Co., 111
Hutchins, Harry, 81, 88, 97, 117
Hyland, Charles, 7

industry and commerce, 3–4, 15, 16,
    18, 25, 26, 49, 50, 58, 70, 71,
    83–84, 94, 111–112, 118, 122–123,
    150, 167; auto, 83, 110–111, 122;
    leather, 3, 43; printing, 18, 50;
    wool, 2–3, 18
Inglis, Agnes, 86

International Radio Corporation, 118
International Research Corporation,
    122
International White Cross, 131
Irish community, 7, 18, 36

Jewish community, 26–27, 49,
    124–125, 150; cemetery, 26, 49
Johnson, Hugh, 80
Johnson Lyndon B., 147–148, 161
juvenile delinquency, 132
Juvenile Temperance Union, 64

Keck, John, 58, 70
Kennedy, John F., 146, 147, 148
King-Seeley Corporation, 111, 122
Kingsley, James, 30, 52
Know Your City, 148
Know Your Town, 148

labor movement, 94, 99, 100, 103,
    120–121, 123
Ladies Library Association, 46
Ladies of Temperance, 11
League of Women Voters, 144, 148
Lewis, George E., 108
Liberty Party, 28
Lincoln, Abraham, 36, 38, 42
Little, Clarence Cook, 113
Local News and Advertiser, 34
Look, 152
Loomis, William and Caroline, 37, 42
Lower Town, 5–6, 8, 13, 25, 27, 40
Lucking, William A., 132, 136

McCreery, William, 7
Mack, Christian, 61
Mack, Walter C., 115
Mackenzie, R.G., 88
McKinley, William, 76
Manley, Charles H., 37
Mann, Jonathan Henry, 6, 21
Mann, Solomon, 19
marijuana ordinance, 161–162
Martin, Oliver, 35

May Festival, 77
Maynard, John, 61
Maynard, William S., 20, 25, 27, 30, 34, 36, 43
Metzger, William, 126
Michigan Age, 104, 105
Michigan Anti-Slavery Society, 28
Michigan Argus, 18, 28, 39, 40
"Michigan fever," 4
Michigan League (U-M), 112–113
Michigan State Journal, 6, 13, 15
Michigan Temperance Herald, 10
Michigan Theater, 100
Michigan Whig, 6, 13
Michiganensian, 150
Misses Clark School for Young Ladies, 15–16, 64
Model Cities Program, 166
Morgan, Elijah, 6, 10, 11, 23, 25, 27, 30, 50
Morgan, Lucy, 4
Morse, Ellen, 58
Mozart Watch Co., 49
Muehlig, Bertha, 113
municipal preservation ordinance, 158
Murphy, Frank, 119, 120, 123
music, 41, 56, 77, 81, 161, 168

National Association for the Advancement of Colored People (NAACP), 142, 151, 152
National Municipal League, 152
Native American Association of Ann Arbor, 18
Neighborhood Rehabilitation and Improvement Committee, 144
New England Society, 16
New York Daily Graphic, 52
New York Society, 17
Newkirk, H. Wirt, 120, 121
Nickels Arcarde, 94
Nixon, Richard M. 146

observatory (U-M), 48, 78, 79
O'Hara, William, 7

Old West Side Association, 158
Olmsted report, 105–108
Opera House, 35, 56

Packard, Benjamin, 3, 11
Panic of 1837, 18
Panic of 1873, 49, 50
Park Commission, 88
parking, traffic, 110, 132, 137, 167
Patton, Carl, 88
Peninsular Courier, 42, 46
Pittsfield Village, 130, 151
police, 22, 48–49, 81, 127, 128, 136, 155–157, 160, 163; black appointed, 80–81; Mutual Protection Society, 23
politics (see also civil rights movement; elections): apathy, 116, 123, 130–131; black vote, 80; fiscal matters, 23, 48–49, 64, 69–71, 85, 88, 116, 138, 152, 163; mayoral recall drive, 157; preferential voting, 165
Pond, Elihu, 39, 48
population (see also census), 3, 7, 10, 16–19, 21, 26–27, 35, 36, 40, 49, 58–60, 64, 74, 79–80, 83, 103, 105, 109, 124, 135, 144, 149–150, 157
Poulos, Angelo, 100
Preketes, Tony, 100
prejudice (see also racism): anti-Catholic, anti-immigrant, 17–18; anti-German, 97–99, 126–127; anti-Jewish, 26
Presbyterian Church, 10, 11, 98
Progressive Party, 85
Prohibition, 100–101; repeal, 123
Prohibition Party, 66, 80
Prohibitionist, 64
prostitution, 67

racism, 28, 41–42, 80, 141–142
Ragland, John, 132
railroad, see transportation
Rainbow People, 160–161

religion, see churches; Jewish community
rent control, see housing
Republicans (see also politics), 36, 66, 80, 109, 138, 146, 153, 154, 161, 165
research, 139–140, 150
Robison, John J., 67
Rominger, Marie, 64
Roosevelt, Franklin D., 117, 121, 123–124, 148
Rose, Preston, 37
Rumsey, Elisha, 1–3, 6, 15

Sadler, Walter C., 123, 136
St. Andrew's Episcopal Church, 48
St. Thomas Catholic Church, 18, 62, 72
saloons, 44–48, 50, 61, 65–67
Sanger, Margaret, 86
Schmid, Friedrich, 6–7, 21
schools, 15, 19, 21, 71, 72, 74, 84–85, 145
Second Baptist Church, 55, 144
Sedgwick, George, 23, 30, 36
Sierra Club, 158
Silk, Julia, 39, 43
Sinclair, John, 160–161
Smith, Al, 117
Social Purity Club, 86
Socialist Party, 117, 121, 165
Soldiers Aid Society of Ann Arbor, 39
Sons of Temperance, 11
South University disturbances, 155–157
Spaulding, W.F., 26
Spanish-American War, 76–77
Staebler, Edward, 111, 116, 118–119, 146
Star Theater riot, 81, 155
Stephenson, James, 165
Steuben Guards, 36, 37
Stevenson, Adlai E., 146
Stone, Mrs. Peter, 118, 120
Stratton, Jonathan F., 13

streets, street repair, 3, 10, 35, 71–72, 79, 105–106, 108, 109–110, 116, 152, 157, 167
Student Lecture Association, 31
Sykes, Samuel, 26

Tappan, Henry Philip, 21, 28–30, 36, 39–40, 46,, 78, 113, 148, 161
teach-in, Vietnam War, 153
temperance movement (see also Prohibition), 10–11, 46–48, 59, 64–67, 123, 150
Tenants Union, 152
Thomas, Norman, 117, 123
transportation: automobile, 89–90, 94, 109–110, 137; bicycle, 74; bus, 163; electric street railway, 71; horse, 10, 90, 109, 132; railroad, 13, 48–49, 55

Union School, 25, 33–34
University of Michigan: Ann Arbor location, 6, 13, 15, 16, 50–51, 57, 79, 108; Comprehensive Building Program (1922), 108–113; eminent domain 50–51, 79; enrollment, 28, 40, 41, 46, 60, 71, 95, 102–103, 108, 135–136, 150, of blacks, 41, of women, 103, 130; football stadium, 108, 147, 154; growth and expansion, 28–33, 48, 56–57, 73–74, 78–79, 122, 138–140; hospitals, 31, 48, 73–74, 79, 88, 108, 136; housing, see U-M students; law school, 30–31, 71, 108, 120; library, 30, 56; medical school, 28, 33, 46, 74; North Campus, 138; observatory, 48, 78, 79; relations with city, see city-university relations; state appropriations, 50–51, 57, 79, 108; University Hall, 50–51
University of Michigan alumni, 79
University of Michigan students: conduct off campus, 32, 44–46, 74–76, 81, 110, 146, 155–157; cultural

organizations, 31; economic status, 40, 57; expulsions, 32, 42–43; foreign, 142, 146; fraternities, 32, 76; off-campus housing, 40, 142; political activity, 36, 42–43, 66, 75–76, 126, 147, 152–157, 160–165; university housing, 29–30, 112–113, 136

University Republican Club, 75
urban renewal, 142–144
utilities: electricity, 64, 70; sewer, 71, 120, 121; water, 64, 70, 88

VanBuren, Martin, 18
VanTyne, Claud, 97
Verschoor, C. A. 122
Veterans' Administration Hospital, 138, 140
Vietnam War, controversy, 153–155
Vogel, Martin, 61

Walker Carriage Works, 58
Wallace, George, 163
Walz, William, 86
Washtenaw County (see also county seat; census): 3, 16, 129–130, 155
Wedemeyer, George, 144, 146
Washtenaw Post, 89, 96
Washtenaw Post Tribune, 129
Weil brothers, 26–27, 49
Weil, Jacob, 27, 36
Wheeler, Albert, 141–142, 165–167

Whig Party, 18, 36
White, Andrew D., 52
White Panthers, see Rainbow People
Widenman, August, 25
Willkie, Wendell, 123
Willow Run Bomber Plant, 129–130
Wilson, Samuel, 80
Wilson, Woodrow, 117
women: economic role, 58–60, 83–84, 94–95, 109, 124; percent of population, 21, 109, 124; university students, 60, 103, 130
Women of the Republic, 103
Women's Christian Temperance Union (WCTU), 64, 66
women's organizations, 11, 86, 94–95, 103, 144, 148
women's suffrage, 59–61, 105
Woodbridge, William, 15
Works Progress Administration, (WPA), 121–122
World War I, 93–102, 128
World War II, 126–132
Wright, George, 105
Wurster, Ernst, 95, 98, 101

Young, Leigh, 128
Young Men's Literary Society, 15
Yuwer, Nicholas, 93–94

Zion Lutheran Church, 6–7, 98, 101
zoning, see city planning